THE CITIZEN DECIDES

RALPH BARTON PERRY

The Citizen Decides

A GUIDE TO RESPONSIBLE
THINKING IN TIME OF CRISIS

INDIANA UNIVERSITY PRESS
BLOOMINGTON   1951

This book is
dedicated with respect and admiration to
the thinking citizens of
THE LEAGUE OF WOMEN VOTERS

PREFACE

THERE ARE many reasons why an American citizen should be troubled at the present time. The problems of American public policy are vast and intricate. In recent decades they have come more and more to embrace technical matters. Even nuclear physics falls within the field of things that the citizen has to think about. And all problems of public policy are now problems of *global* policy.

It is possible to evade these difficulties, and not think at all or borrow the ready-made opinions of others. This is the line of least resistance. But it does not agree with the idea of a democracy, in which the final authority is public opinion, and in which public opinion is supposed to be the product of freedom and enlightenment.

The citizen has heavy obligations as well as difficult problems. The present book is a confession of my own experience. I find myself compelled to think about many things of which I have no knowledge, and my conscience as a citizen goads me into making decisions when it would be far easier to remain in doubt or

evade the issue altogether. In the later chapters of
the book I have stated some of these decisions in the
area of foreign policy, lest I seem to be a preacher,
and not a practicer, of my gospel.

I am grateful to Manley O. Hudson, Zechariah
Chafee, Bishop John J. Wright and others, for an-
swering my questions; to Ruth Kingsberg and Con-
stance R. McClellan for secretarial assistance; and to
Elizabeth P. Aldrich for reading and correcting my
manuscript.

RALPH BARTON PERRY

Cambridge, Massachusetts
July 16, 1951

TABLE OF CONTENTS

[*ix*]

Contents

[x]

Contents

of conflicting interests. The divorce of government, law, and business from morality.

The present global situation. Different stages of advancement in human societies. The revolt against colonialism. The rise of the proletariat. The appeal of Communism. Democracy advocates gradualism *vs* violent revolution. The United States and the world revolution.

War not inevitable. The justification of war. The evil of war. The purpose of peace and security. The logic of war and the logic of peace. The view of General MacArthur.

Short-range and long-range policy. The four fronts of foreign policy. Diplomacy and politics. Diplomacy and bad manners. The menace of Soviet Russia. American policy in the Far East. Military armament. Universal military training.

Propaganda and the Voice of America. The American appeal *vs* the appeal of Soviet Russia. The weakness and the strength of our appeal. Programs for world development.

The division of the world. The ultimate ideal of human brotherhood.

THE CITIZEN DECIDES

CHAPTER I

PITY THE POOR CITIZEN!

Should we send wheat to India?" "Whom will the
Republicans nominate for the presidency in
1952?" "What did you think of MacArthur's
speech?" "Should we start a preventive war against
Russia?" "Should Acheson be fired?" "Should the
farmers be given parity?" "Should Congress pass an
anti-lynching bill?" "Should we adopt socialized
medicine?" "Should we adopt universal military
training?" "Should taxes be increased?" "Should Communist China be admitted to the United Nations?"
"Should the boys be sent to Europe?" "Should Communists be allowed to teach?"

Such questions, liberally interspersed with non-
political questions such as "Will the Yankees beat the
Red Sox?" and "How's business?" provide topics of
conversation whenever two or three Americans are
gathered together. These conversations are not limited to highbrows, or to those who have had a "college education": they occur among travelling sales-
men in the smoking compartments of railway trains,
among house painters on the scaffolding, between

any man and his taxi driver, or among farmers at the country store. They represent the kind of opinions that American citizens are called upon to have, and one of the ways in which American opinion is made and spread.

It is sometimes supposed that the citizen has discharged his political obligations when he has voted, and that he deserves special credit if he drives somebody else to the polls. But voting is the least arduous of a citizen's duties. He has the prior and harder duty of making up his mind. As election day approaches, he has to decide *how* to vote, and in season and out he has to decide what to think. His private opinion, when put together with the opinions of others like him, is public opinion; and public opinion is the ultimate force which, in America, governs policy and political action.

This control by public opinion is an essential part of what we mean by democracy. The citizen, as conceived by the founding fathers, is not merely an advocate of his own interests and those of his class; he is a judge of what is best for everybody. A recent writer has said that whereas our democracy is "government of the people, by the people, for the people," the Russian idea is "government for the people with the consent of the people." [1] The people of Russia, according to this writer, are incapable of agreeing among themselves and require that some sort of doctrine shall be imposed on them from above or outside—for their own good. But independent political thinking is the crux of popular sovereignty, as we understand that principle. It is not sufficient that the citizen should "consent." A political system in which public opinion is manufactured by the rulers, so that the people merely give back the opinion which has been handed out to them, is not a government by the people, any more than applause can be said to represent the ideas of the audience.

When the American colonists rejected the British king, they did not substitute an aristocracy or even a parliament: they substituted themselves. "Uneasy lies the head that wears a crown"—in a democracy every responsible citizen wears a crown, and will suffer that uneasiness. Most of the major changes in our political procedures have confirmed this idea, both in theory and in practice. It has proved acceptable not only to political philosophers, but to the average American's instinctive dislike of being "told" what is good for him. He likes to manage his own affairs and make up his own mind.

It is, of course, true that even in a democracy, American model, most people most of the time have their minds made up by somebody else. The more thoughtful men and women, or the leaders in various walks of life, or the speakers and writers, formulate opinions and spread them abroad. Members of religious sects, political parties, and economic groups have their opinions largely made for them before they

[5]

are born, or at least before they become politically conscious. But even so, opinions begin *somewhere,* and they are unaccountably altered as they pass from mind to mind.

In these days there are "experts" in everything: experts engaged in scientific research, and experts whose services can be obtained by payment of a fee. There are experts in "public relations." Psychologists and sociologists devote much attention to the processes of opinion-making; politicians, journalists and "pollsters" venture both to analyze and to predict the state of the public mind. Their failures are as notable as their successes. The "how" of public opinion—how an opinion gets crystallized and spread to the point at which it becomes "public"—is still a mystery. This is probably because there are so many causes, and because the operation of *deciding,* which goes on in each individual mind, is so inscrutable. Who can tell just how he came to choose his wife or his occupation? And yet these are simple decisions as compared with the weighing of the pro's and con's that enter into a political decision. But without attempting any general solution of this problem, it is possible to name some of the factors involved and some of the difficulties which beset the citizen who tries to do his own political thinking.

The citizen of today is called upon to decide questions of great diversity and complexity. Economic questions, for example, have become at the same time more complicated and more political. There have always been economic-political issues before the public mind—the national bank, the conflict between manufacturing and agrarian interests, the inflation of the currency, and the tariff. But with the first administration of Franklin Roosevelt, new problems arose and old problems were aggravated: employment, labor relations, the gold standard, government regulation of business, foreign trade, "parity," monopoly, the increase of the national debt—these and a dozen other questions became matters on which political parties wrote platforms, and on which economists wrote controversial books, and on which the bewildered voter was supposed to decide.

And now the vast problems of international relations have been added to all these questions: war hot and war cold, world government, and foreign policy, both general and regional. The citizen needs to have a map of the globe constantly at his side. He must know the islands of the Pacific and the backward and dependent areas of the Far East. He must know the difference between the Balkans and the Baltics, and between Iran and Iraq. He must learn the boundaries of Kashmir and Ceylon, and penetrate behind the barriers of the Himalayas to the once inaccessible Tibet. Without such knowledge he cannot read his morning paper (except the comics and the sporting page); and he cannot converse with his neighbor (except on matters of personal gossip).

[7]

In short, the immense responsibility in world affairs, which America has more or less reluctantly assumed, now rests with the American citizen. He must become "globally minded." World affairs are not entrusted to a learned ruling class, because world affairs have become matters of American policy and because those who determine and administer American policy are guided by what they think American citizens think. There is always an impending election for which the politicians begin to prepare before the echoes of the last election have died away. All branches of government—the two houses of Congress, the Executive, and even (though more remotely) the Judiciary—take their cue from public opinion. Officials hear from their constituents. The Department of State, entrusted with the delicate task of negotiation with other governments, is watched, criticized, rebuked, and even threatened with impeachment, by those who speak in the name of the people. Diplomats are often the prisoners of the public opinion which they have themselves helped to create, and which has got beyond their control. The outcome of international conferences between heads of government, and hence the fate of the world, is linked with the grass-roots of opinion of America.

The American citizen is not kept in the dark. The arts of communication, of which television is the latest manifestation, leave nothing of privacy or secrecy or remoteness; but create an immense revolving

[8]

searchlight which lays bare every leaf on every tree of every forest, however distant. Publicity is both telescopic and microscopic. The making of policy takes place before the camera and in the glare of neon lights. Officials of government are subjected to frequent interviews by a press which they dare not offend; and the demands of public talking often leave little time for private thinking. Not only officials, but individuals who would like to be "private individuals," are haled before investigating committees and threatened with "contempt" if they do not reveal their innermost thoughts. Events are made known instantly, and sometimes when they have not even occurred, to the listening ears of a nation-wide radio audience. Journals, magazines and pocket books are piled high on the newsstands; pamphlets and mimeographed circulars clog the mails. There is, in short, a plethora of somewhat dubious information and highly dubious opinion. The problem for the citizen is not how to fill his head, but how to keep it.

The modern American press surpasses that of any other time or place at both ends of the scale: its best newspapers are the best, and its worst are the worst. Its correspondents travel to all parts of the world, and an immense volume of news, arriving by cable, telegraph, and telephone, is immediately distributed to millions of readers—at the cost of the advertisers. "News" is supposed to be divorced from "opinion," but news has to be selected, summarized and headlined, so that the reader who "glances" at his paper at the breakfast table, or on his way to the office, has his news largely predigested for him. A newspaper can convey its opinion with the least resistance by conveying it in the form of "slanted" news. But the almost insuperable task of filtering the facts from the news is given to the poor citizen.

Yet even if the citizen were completely informed, that would not suffice. It is necessary to form an opinion "in the light of the facts." Arguments have to be "weighed," and after "both sides have been heard" and "all things considered," a decision has to be reached. When opinions are borrowed, the reliability of their source has to be assessed.

Opinions abound and they are freely aired. Columnists, commentators, editorial writers, and speakers heard over the radio or reported in the press, all advocate their views. But this only aggravates the problem of the citizen. It is easy to make up your mind in the presence of one opinion, or even two, but it becomes increasingly difficult in proportion to their number and diversity. There is a widely accepted fiction that the truth is somehow revealed in a clash of opinions: nothing could be further from the truth. A mere clash of opinions is deafening and blinding, and the victim is glad to take refuge in the quiet of evasion, dogma, or scepticism. That "market of ideas" to which Justice Holmes was willing to entrust the emergence of truth resembles the floor of the stock exchange in a day of panic. It has no kinship with the "sessions of sweet silent thought."

Even when men are well-informed, disinterested and reasonably reasonable, political decisions are immensely difficult. There are many variables. The right is rarely, if *ever*, all on one side—there is usually "something to be said" for the other. And whichever side one takes, one will find strange bedfellows with whom one would prefer not to agree.

The decisive rôle of public opinion in American policy, and the influences which darken and confuse the public mind, place a peculiar responsibility on the so-called "educated classes," and upon those citizens with courage enough to assume responsibility. I am not naïve or optimistic enough to suppose that the majority of American citizens are thinking citizens. Nor do I believe that there is any infallible wisdom to be found in mass non-thinking, provided only the mass is large enough. The problems of public affairs are solved, so far as they are solved, by a thinking minority, whose conclusions are endorsed by others. But while independent political thinking is not a correct description, it is the proper standard, of American citizenship. The *idea* of the American political system is realized only when such thinking is widely diffused; moreover, it must be raised to a high level of intelligence and disinterestedness in the minds of those who are most favored by nature and opportunity.

Conditions being what they are at the present time, it is small wonder that Americans, educated and uneducated alike, are grateful for headlines, clichés, slogans, and any other kind of tabloid opinion which will simplify the issues of the day, save them the labor of thinking, and replace ideas with emotional attitudes which require no evidence beyond the fact that most other people appear to feel the same way.

CHAPTER II

IS OUR SIDE ALWAYS RIGHT?

No one who sees the propaganda film depicting the great meeting of the Nazi Party in Nuremberg in 1934 can fail to be deeply disturbed. That which is disturbing is not the aspect of the leaders, for Hitler, Goebbels, Goering, Streicher, Hess *et al.* are not personally impressive; quite the contrary—it is evident that they were putting on a show, and were childishly pleased with their success. No, the terrifying thing is not that there should be such vicious leaders, but that acres of their betters, marching in uniform or applauding the spectacle from the sidelines, should have been excited to such a frenzy of submissiveness. Without a trace of hate or cynicism, they wear expressions of ecstatic adoration on their faces. Adoration of what?—of an abstraction called *Deutschland*. Adoration of whom?—of a little man of insignificant appearance and inflated vanity.

It is impossible to witness this spectacle without a feeling of guilt at finding oneself so moved by its mass and rhythm; and without a feeling that even Americans, with their supposedly incorrigible individualism, independence, and sense of humor, might joyfully surrender their liberties and cross that short emotional interval that divides a demagogue from a demigod. Indeed it is said that the showing of this film is restricted owing to the fear that American audiences might be too responsive to its appeal. Is that fear ungrounded? Or do we share that fear—"there but for the grace of God go we"? "It might happen here?" Or *does* it happen here?

The fact is that there is something in this behavior which is so human that no human group can boast itself invulnerable. All human groups have exhibited this behavior, in advanced as well as in primitive societies. The development of science has not in the least diminished it; on the contrary, it has provided it with new instruments by which its effects are intensified and more widely extended. Furthermore, this behavior is manifested in great moments of human experience; not in war only, but in games and festivals, in religious worship and in patriotism.

Patriotism is one of the loftiest and at the same time one of the most dangerous emotions of which mankind is capable. The feeling which binds men to those who live under a common government, with whom they share a common tradition and common ideals, is an indispensable condition of survival. It represents the fundamental fact that men must stand together for defense against enemies, that they must do together those things which lie beyond their powers as isolated individuals or families. For many this sentiment is the highest motive which they ever know, inducing them to sacrifice their private gain and even their lives to the general good. Those who have not risen to the level of patriotism are not likely to rise to higher levels. The fact that patriotism has its excesses and abuses is no reason to make light of it. He who "never to himself hath said, 'This is my own, my native land!' " is as unnatural as the mother who has no invincible attachment to her child. The larger and more generous loyalties are built upon those more intimate and instinctive loyalties which nature has provided.

The evil of patriotism, as well as its good, is embodied in the utterance "my country, right or wrong." Here is devotion and fidelity, but also a disregard of principle. If patriotism is "the last refuge of a scoundrel," it is not merely because evil deeds may be performed in the *name* of patriotism and covered by its cloak, but because patriotic fervor can obliterate moral distinctions altogether; it can declare a general moratorium on moral obligations, and overwhelm the more decent and humane propensities. Short of the last desperate extremity of self-preservation, there is another and better patriotism in which "my country" is loved for what it means—for the values which it symbolizes and to which it is dedicated.

The evil of patriotism, then, lies in *sheer* patriotism—or in that impulse which induces men to take

"our side" merely because it is "ours." In a comparatively innocent sphere of life, competitive sports,
there is the attitude of those who cheer for victory,
their mind being intent only on the score. There is
another attitude, not to be expected of the "rooter,"
which applauds skill and esteems scrupulous observance of the rules. Similarly, we suppose that a country
"stands for something," and that America stands for
democracy. Naked partisanship ignores that which
the country stands for, and tends to divorce emotion
from ideas and ideals.

Every victory is at the same time a defeat and to
will the one is to will the other. Those who cheer also jeer. In sports, this negative attitude can be sub-
limated in love of the game. But antagonism between
nations is not a game—the defeat of the opponent is
an end in itself. If love is good for the soul, so hate,
by the same token, is corrupting and debasing.

To use again the analogy of sports, it is to be noted
that members of the cheering section cast sidelong
glances at one another, and that they may even employ more palpable threats against those who fail to
cheer. Emotional patriotism becomes a club by which
dissident or apathetic individuals are brought into
conformity. The accusation of disloyalty needs no
other evidence than a hesitation to cheer or shout
with the crowd, and needs no other penalty than to
be labeled an outcast. As patriotism becomes a protective coloration by which the individual's behavior

in other respects escapes notice, so the dissenter, however slight his deviation, becomes a marked man from whom others withdraw themselves. Patriotism is converted into the persecution of those who are deemed nonpatriotic by the patriots. The more passionate the patriotism, the closer the scrutiny and the quicker the suspicion.

As patriotism becomes passionate and partisan, that self-criticism which is essential to social and political progress becomes proportionately inhibited. Love of country becomes love of the *status quo*. When innovation is considered unpatriotic, the unfamiliar is considered alien. Strangers and foreigners are suspected. All the phobias—Anglophobia, Francophobia and the rest—find the climate congenial, and develop into a general xenophobia. The result is usually a bigoted provincialism, which is not only contrary to the hospitality which a democracy such as America has traditionally extended to all mankind, but cuts off the flow of influences from abroad by which American culture has been historically enriched.

The cause of patriotic excesses is to be found in the fact that emotions acquire a life of their own and grow by what they feed on. There are certain powerful impulses in human nature which ordinarily play the rôle of auxiliary forces that can be harnessed to any end. Of these the most notable are fear and rage. An American philosopher-psychologist calls them "injectives," [1] because they inject energy into other impulses. They stimulate the adrenal glands, and flood the system with augmented power. They are like high explosives, with which one can either clear a channel for commerce, or destroy a city. When these impulses are strong enough, they sweep us away altogether. We then revel in the immediate satisfactions which fear and rage themselves provide; and for the sake of these satisfactions, fear and rage invent their own objects. They pass from one man to another by a sort of contagion, and may take possession of a whole social group. When this reaches a certain point, we call it "hysteria" or "panic."

In other words, the emotions of fear and rage instead of being our servants can become our masters. When under control, they strengthen our power to escape evil or overcome it; when they assume control, they may bring about a displacement or even an inversion of values. Fear and rage against the infidel have sometimes transformed Christians into marauding crusaders or into inquisitors and persecutors, guilty of the utmost cunning and cruelty. The friends of freedom have been transformed by fear and rage into the instruments of slavery. The enemies of a reign of terror have been known to use the harshest intimidation in opposing it.

The evil that fear and rage can do when they take possession of men, and expel both humanity and thought from the human mind, appears in the behavior both of mobs and of persons. "McCarthyism" and "MacArthurism" have many contributing causes, but in some degree the first is the effect of unreasoning suspicion, and the second of unreasoning combativeness.

For the dehumanizing effect of uncontrolled rage and inveterate hatred, one does not have to search the history of primitive or savage tribes. It was in Germany, and of recent date, that Jewish infants were denied the use of milk in order that they might die of starvation. Nearer home, we are familiar with our own vigilantes and lynchers, and the sadistic pleasure which they appear to enjoy.

The behavior of the mob is the human conduct most difficult to reconcile with the idea of a benevolent Creator—even war has, or once had, its "Don't cheer, boys; the poor devils are dying." To account for man's brutality to man, Satan had to be invented —a Satan whom even the Creator could not forgive. But unhappily it is not necessary to look beyond human nature itself for the explanation. The outbreak of native instincts, out of control, and intensified by numbers, is capable of degrading men to a level of which it is libelous to accuse the beast.

Although fear in its outward manifestations appears to be the opposite of rage, these two impulses are closely interrelated at the center. Fear is convertible into rage, not because it affords a last extremity of escape, but because fear itself enrages, especially

[*19*]

when the object of fear is only vaguely apprehended and when there is no clear means of dealing with it.

The actress Ethel Waters, in her grim and moving autobiography, describes an incident in which she and another girl were pinned under an automobile wreck, severely injured. A white passer-by declined to help, with the words, "The more dead niggers there are, the better I like it." Miss Waters has her explanation of the persecution of which she was a victim:

What could be more pitiful than to live in such night-marish terror of another race that you have to lynch them, push them off sidewalks, and never be able to relax your venomous hatred for one moment? As I see it, it is these people, the Ku-Kluxers, the White Supremacists, and the other fire-spitting neurotics who are in the deep trouble.[2]

But fear has its own corruption and, like rage, becomes an obsession. It then needs no social contagion to give it power. That shrewd analyst of human nature, Plutarch, wrote of a certain great man:

After Alexander had once lost his confidence and become suspicious and easily alarmed, there was no circumstance so trivial that he did not make an omen of it, and the palace was full of sacrifice, lustrations, and soothsayers. So terrible a thing is disbelief in the gods and contempt for them on the one hand, while superstition and excessive reverence for them presses on men's guilty consciences like a torrent of water poured upon them. Thus was Alexander's mind filled with base and cowardly alarms.[3]

Such are the violent manifestations of obsessive emotion. More subtle and insidious are the inner *attitudes* which may be generated and spread by the same causes. The behavior of an invisible "public" may closely parallel the behavior of a visible crowd. Those who read the same press or listen to the same radio broadcast may come under the spell of the same emotional appeal, and feel themselves to be in one another's presence. The audiences of television, with their attention focused simultaneously on the same trial or congressional "investigation," are subject to a kind of hypnosis which dulls their critical faculties and absorbs them into a Great Audience which, although imaginary, intensifies their attitudes. The effect is multiplied by press, newsreels, and illustrated magazines when they repeat the same theme. A total society may "see red," being pervaded by convulsions of rage or panic fear from which no individual dare detach himself lest he direct these emotions to himself.

This is something new in human life—a new form of mental solidarity, both for good and for evil, one of the major threats to the integrity of the thinking individual, and a grave menace to democracy. Its gravity lies in the fact that it can occur in an "orderly" society, and that it transfers the behavior of the mob, once restricted to the capacity of an auditorium or an immediate locality, to the limitless millions

[*21*]

who lie within the range of modern instruments of communication.

Since these forces are capable of being harnessed to any end, they can be manipulated. In the background is usually to be found the sinister figure of the man who coolly generates the heat—the man who sets the stage, or writes the script, or regulates the soundtrack. He is called "Goebbels," let us say. Or he may be called by less evil-sounding names—"propagandist," "director of public relations," "morale builder." He escapes condemnation because the methods which he misuses are similar to those which are used for good.

The oldest name for this manipulator of mass emotion is "demagogue." His methods have remained essentially the same throughout the ages, and have been frequently described, from antiquity to modern times. The great demagogue combines the rôles of playwright and actor. He brings tears to the eyes of the many, or plays upon their fears, or excites them to anger, for calculated reasons of his own, or perhaps to minister to his ego. The superlative demagogue will not only manage, he will also participate. A tear will glisten in his own eye, and there will be a sob in his own voice as well as in the throats of his victims. He will impersonate the anger or the fear which he generates in others, and, moved by his own moving utterances, he will create the impression of sincerity.

Modern technology has given the demagogue new weapons and a wider range of influence. If one is to judge by America, it has also brought a corrective. Americans have created the modern art of advertising, and are familiar with both ends of the operation. They are at once its victims and its agents. They also know how to protect themselves against it. It is characteristically American to have invented a whole vocabulary of derision with which to deflate bombast and sentimentality and supply the antidote of laughter.

How widely this cure is effective is not clear. How many people apply such terms as "ham," "corny," "tripe," "drip," or "out-Barrymore Barrymore" to eloquence that is too transparently designed to create an effect, or too shallow in its appeal? Only the highbrow and the sophisticated? Or is it felt instinctively by the people at large? Is such derision resented by the masses as a sign of snobbery? Whatever the case, the fact remains that demagoguery on all levels, be it skillful or naïve, is made a more and not a less formidable enemy to political thinking by the modern spread of literacy and communication.

In a memorable figure of speech, Plato represents the human soul as composed of a charioteer and two winged horses:

The human charioteer drives his [winged horses] in a pair; and one of them is noble and of noble breed, and the other is ignoble and of ignoble breed; and the driving of

them of necessity gives a great deal of trouble to him. . . .
The right-hand horse is upright and cleanly made; . . . he
is a lover of honour and modesty and temperance, and the
follower of true glory; he needs no touch of the whip, but
is guided by word and admonition only. The other is a
crooked lumbering animal, put together anyhow; he is
flat-faced and of a dark colour, with grey and blood-shot
eyes; the mate of insolence and pride, shag-eared and deaf,
hardly yielding to whip and spur.[4]

Plato's right-hand horse is passion for the good: the
mind moved by love. While the left-hand horse needs
to be curbed, the better horse is the ally of the charioteer, helping him both to subdue the unruly mate
and to reach the goal.

The nobler horse may be taken as symbolizing that
enthusiasm which is indispensable to social action.
Enthusiasm may be taken to mean not sheer unregu-
lated emotion, the servant of every base appetite
which is capable of kicking over the traces and
taking the bit into its teeth—not the runaway emotion
—but emotion inclined to general ends and quickly
responsive to the guidance of reason.

CHAPTER III

CLICHÉS, LABELS, AND MISNOMERS

The duty of the American citizen to think and decide for himself amidst the bewildering complexity of public affairs is rendered difficult not only by the blinding effect of emotion, but by the ambiguity and meaninglessness of words.[1] Words, which we always think of as the tools of thought, are also means of escaping its pains. "I dislike most slogans," Nehru has said. "They prevent the person from thinking."[2] One is tempted to say that the more familiar words and phrases become the more they lose that definite reference to things and ideas for which they were intended. They are worn smooth and indecipherable, like coins which have been long in circulation; and they owe their vogue largely to this fact.

People accept and pass familiar words by habit, or as expressions of emotional attitudes.[3] There is, therefore, a close connection between verbal expressions and the contamination of thought by emotion. Certain words become the effective stimuli by which ready-made emotional reactions of combativeness, sym-

[25]

pathy with the underdog, hero-worship, or hatred are released and propagated. The purpose of the present chapter is to examine and, if possible, to clarify the most familiar of these linguistic obscurities.

There are certain preliminary generalizations that will be illustrated in detail as we proceed. Many of the terms considered are "weapons," calculated to express and win a favorable or unfavorable opinion. Sometimes the same word is used in a favorable sense by one party, and in an unfavorable sense by the opposite party. Closely connected with this double-talk is the practice of hurling back the epithet received. It is customary, and not unusual or absurd, for the pot to call the kettle black, and *vice versa*. When any favorable term is used, or when any ambiguous term is given a favorable meaning, the illustrations cited to explain it are taken from one's own practices, while unfavorable meanings are illustrated only by the opponent's actions. Thus, the so-called *Agitator's Handbook*, published in Moscow, and containing a dictionary of current political terms, illustrates "aggression" by the policy of capitalistic countries, and "intervention" by the aid given to the Russian counter-revolution by the Allies in 1917-20; but "democracy" is illustrated by the "people's democracies" of Soviet Russia and the satellite countries.[4]

Most clichés have a simple emotional meaning and a complex objective meaning. It is for this reason that they have the labor-saving effect of oversimplifying the issue. And finally, many of the terms commonly employed acquire an unfavorable meaning from the addition of the syllable "ism," which usually converts an emotional meaning into an objectionably extreme or doctrinaire meaning; e.g., social: socialism; and military: militarism, etc.

It will be convenient to classify the words and phrases here considered into five groups, which reveal the different contexts in which they are ordinarily employed. Thus, there are words and phrases which concern (1) foreign policy; (2) domestic policy; (3) domestic reactions to foreign policy; (4) evaluations (usually unfavorable) of the opponent; (5) evaluations (usually favorable) of the United States.

At the present time, foreign policy is in the forefront of discussion, and in such discussion the word which leads all the rest in its power to win immediate agreement and silence opposition is the word *appeasement*. This word acquired its vogue and its evil reputation when Neville Chamberlain failed to appease Hitler in 1937. If he had succeeded, perhaps "appeasement" would have become a good instead of a bad word in the vocabulary of international politics.

In its root-meaning, to appease is to pacify, and there can be no harm in that. In a secondary meaning, to appease is to satisfy an appetite or demand—and no one complains of that. In international relations, it is taken to mean the satisfaction of a rival's demand in the hope of obtaining some satisfaction from him in return. When no equivalent or greater benefit is received for a benefit given, the appeasement is proven to have been foolish. It is foolish to appease the unappeasable, or to make concessions which merely increase the opponent's demands; it is this which Senator Vandenberg had in mind when he said that "appeasement is surrender on the installment plan." [5]

It is also foolish to appease from sheer weakness, because one then has no bargaining power—no concessions to make in return for concessions received. Appeasement partakes of something worse than folly when that which one gives up belongs to someone else, or when the giving of it involves the breach of an agreement with a friendly ally. There is a *limit* to what should be conceded in order to appease: one will not surrender one's security or betray certain basic moral principles which one considers inviolable. All of these considerations apply to the appeasement of Munich, which was unsuccessful and dishonorable.

But clearly the fact that there can be bad appeasements does not imply that appeasement cannot be good. This confusion is a serious matter since it discredits the settlement of international disputes by negotiation; that is, by mutual concessions. Since diplomats and other exponents of foreign policy profess to be engaged in a peaceful adjustment of conflicting interests and are at the same time afraid of being called "appeasers," their logic and their rhetoric do not run together. For example, in his address before the National Association of Radio and Television Broadcasters on April 17, 1951, General Bradley said (applauded, no doubt, by the audience), "There is one price we will not pay—appeasement." Then, in a later passage, he said, "Our best chance for the survival of our way of life, and our freedom is to continue coöperation in mutual security efforts, and to *continue negotiation* in this world-wide conflict as long as possible." [6] But what does that mean if not a willingness to make concessions to the other nation's demands in order to obtain concessions in return?

There is evidence that American statesmen are becoming increasingly aware that it is desirable to make the meaning of appeasement more explicit. In his address to the Women's National Press Club on April 18, 1951, the Secretary of State rejected the "extreme view" that "any willingness to settle the problems of Korea by peaceful means is tantamount to appeasement." Later he said, "To end the fighting by giving the aggressor what he seeks would be appeasement in *the true sense of the word*." It would hardly do to say in general that in a conflict of interest the opponent must never be conceded that, or any part of that, for which he takes or makes a good deal of trouble. This would be to exclude from negotiation the very crux of the issue—that which makes negotiation necessary. It would be difficult, for example, to apply this notion of appeasement to a dispute between labor and employer. It might also exclude the appeasement of its Republican opponents by a Democratic administration. In any case, what Secretary Acheson meant became clear in a later paragraph of the above address, in which he said, "*Aggression* cannot be allowed to succeed; *it* cannot be appeased, rewarded or ignored. To meet it squarely is the price of peace." [7]

This appears to be the view sanctioned by President Truman: "To reach . . . a settlement, the Soviet and Chinese Communist leaders must abandon their aggression. On that point there can be no compromise. *We will not engage in appeasement.* We will make no deals that would reward aggression." [8] It is to be noted that the President does not say that there must be no dealing with "aggressors," for, since the Chinese Communists have been so named, that would exclude dealing with the very party with whom we desire to reach a settlement. The point of the contention is that an aggressor must not be conceded *that for which* he committed aggression.

Thus, the odium is shifted to aggression, and to its passive acceptance. The term "appeasement" serves no rational purpose. It retains only a rhetorical force, which is the reason, no doubt, why it is so often used when it adds nothing to the meaning of the argument. But like so many emotional terms it can be misused—that is, used to persuade people to abandon negotiation and resort to action. It is now the handiest stick with which political opponents beat the Department of State, and with which those who talk war beat those who talk of peace. In a parody of *Alice in Wonderland* by James Reston, the Hatter says, "Appeasement's the trouble. That's what causes the confusion. When you get into any kind of war you must use all the power you have; otherwise you're an appeaser." Whereupon Alice (the troubled citizen!) says that she supposes "that's what we should have done with the Russians when they blockaded Berlin and with the Jugoslavs when they shot down the American planes. . . ." [9]

"Appeasement" merely befogs the issue. Instead of the maxim, "Thou shalt not appease," I would propose the maxim, "Thou shalt not use the word 'appeasement.' "

The dictionary meaning of *aggression* is "unprovoked attack," or "the first attack." As applied to international affairs, the idea of non-provocation has become subordinated to the idea of crossing some established political frontier with an armed force first, whatever the provocation. In its most aggravated form, it means armed invasion for the purpose of territorial gain, but since all wars now tend to become disastrous in their effects, the motive has become less important. The evil thing is to *start* a war.

Hence the North Koreans are termed "aggressors" because they first crossed the Thirty-eighth Parallel, regardless of the fact that the South Koreans appear to have harbored similar intentions. Attributing aggression to the North Koreans also implies that a provisional frontier is still a frontier provided there are different governments on its opposite sides. It would seem to follow that, as the political division between Communist and Nationalist China becomes stabilized, an invasion of Formosa from the continent or of the continent from Formosa would be an aggression.

Whether aggression is or is not illegal is a question that cannot be answered with exactness. Only one thing is clear; namely, that it is illegal *in terms of the Charter of the United Nations.* Its position with regard to international law is in the making. Moreover, aggression is clearly contrary to "the conscience of mankind"; no nation commits it without indignantly denying that it is doing so. When first North Korea, and then Communist China, were "branded" as aggressors, this moral sentiment was invoked.

When this "branding" was executed by the United Nations, it was considered not only as the condemning of a breach of the peace, but as an application of the principle of *collective security.* "What we call collective security," Secretary Acheson has said, "is the willingness of nations to fight side by side, if necessary, for the safety of any of them because their common safety is involved." [10] If this definition is accepted, it would apply to any mutual defense treaty, or to a coalition, such as that formed by the European nations against Napoleon.

There is, however, another conception which tends to give the idea of collective security a greater moral and legal force. According to this conception, collective security means that the members of a community agree among themselves not only to prevent, but also to *refrain* from breaking the peace. When collective security is thus interpreted (as a mutual compact), the member of the United Nations which breaks the peace has also broken an agreement, and is guilty in a double sense.

In view of the fact that North Korea and Communist China were not members of the United Nations, their "branding" has perhaps been somewhat overplayed. It is true that the Charter provides that "'the Organization shall ensure that states which are not members of the United Nations act in accordance with [its] principles so far as may be necessary for the maintenance of international peace and security." [11] But, to quote a comment on this Article, "the Charter does not create any legal obligations for states not Members of the Organization. They are therefore not obligated in a legal sense to act according to the Principles of the Charter for any purpose whatsoever. The Charter system therefore provides for the imposition, by force if necessary, of the prescribed conduct without legal basis in contractual agreement." [12]

There has been some confusion on this point. Whatever the merit of the question otherwise, if admitted to the United Nations, Communist China would at once assume a legal obligation to refrain from aggression, and to participate in measures taken for collective security. Otherwise, the guilt of Communist China must be conceived as an injury to mankind through aggravating the evils of war, or through violating the moral code of peace-loving mankind.

When the United Nations was first proposed and its provisions were being drafted, there was much talk about *sovereignty*. There is an apparent contradiction between "the principle of sovereign equality" affirmed in the Charter and submission to the Charter as binding on the member-states. There *is* a contradiction, provided sovereignty is taken as absolute. No doubt this misunderstanding was necessary if the United Nations was to be politically acceptable to the major powers at the time, for, whatever else it might mean, sovereignty was something which those who had it were not disposed to "surrender."

People have now become accustomed to the idea that sovereignty is a matter of degree, and may be given up in some respects and retained in others; and to the idea that a sovereign state, in the exercise of its sovereignty, may *delegate* some fraction of its sovereignty. As to sovereign "equality," there is no difficulty, provided it means that the members are equally sovereign, however much or little sovereignty they may possess; and provided it is recognized that states which are equal in the degree of their sovereignty may be unequal in power and influence.

Intervention is also a term that must not be too strictly interpreted. The use of the regular military establishment against either party in a civil or external war is aggression; except when done by authority of the United Nations in pursuance of its pacific purpose. It was this exception which provided the ground of the contention that the American intervention in Korea was legal intervention, whereas the intervention of Communist China was illegal. But there are other kinds of intervention which are more dubious, such as the shipment of American supplies to Britain for use against Germany in 1939-1940. Or military aid to a belligerent may be given in the form of "volunteers," or of military commissions, such as the one sent by the United States to Formosa.

All the doubts and confusions attending the idea of intervention were conspicuous at the time of the Spanish Civil War. Twenty-seven nations, including Germany and Italy, agreed to participate in a "nonintervention" conference in London in 1936. It was a notorious fact that regular Italian troops in considerable numbers were sent to Spain to support Franco, but it was claimed that these were volunteers, and the same claim was made for the aid given to Franco by Germany and to the Loyalists by Russia. Even the United States had its Lincoln Brigade. England, France and the United States were accused of intervening in behalf of Franco because they banned the normal sale of supplies to the recognized régime. In short, the term "intervention" is capable of so many shades of meaning that it is doubtful if it serves any useful purpose in present political thinking.

Dissatisfaction with the Charter of the United Nations has centered on the requirement for unanimity among the Permanent Members when voting on other than procedural questions in the Security Council. This gives to the United States, the United Kingdom, Soviet Russia, France and "China" a right of "veto," of which Soviet Russia has made frequent use to prevent action approved by a majority of the Council. Convinced that the United Nations as now organized is unable to realize its primary purpose of averting war, groups of American citizens have proposed to amend the Charter or to establish a new organization in its place. The diversity of these proposed remedies has given rise to considerable confusion.[13]

The expression *world government* is sometimes used loosely to embrace every form of international organization, including the United Nations itself. Or, more strictly, it may be reserved for the creation of a supreme over-all political authority to which all "citizens of the world" would owe allegiance, which would have its own world legislature, its own body of law, and a power of enforcement which, within its area of jurisdiction, would overrule that of existing national governments. But it is more in accordance with existing American usage to use "world-government" to refer to any plan which would move *in the direction* of a world-government in the stricter sense of the term. Of these plans there are four which have become familiar to the American public.*

The *American Association for the United Nations* (A. A. U. N.) emphasizes the achievements and possibilities of the United Nations, opposes alternative plans as tending to diminish the prestige of the United Nations, and advocates popular education on

---

*The diversity of ideas in this field of political thought and action is by no means exhausted by this list. There are, for example, those who would reject the United Nations or any other form of international organization. Some would revert to isolation; others such as James Burnham, Herman Finer, and Henry R. Luce, advocate, more or less avowedly, an American imperialism. In Europe, with headquarters in London, there are those who propose to short-circuit the United Nations, or any other inter-governmental organization, by a People's World Convention. The Progressive Party plan (as formulated by Henry A. Wallace) and the plan of the American Friends Service Committee (cf. its booklet, entitled *The United States and the Soviet Union*) agree in emphasizing pacific and economic measures rather than the use of military force. The World's Peace Congress, initiated by Soviet Russia and considered "subversive" in America, attempts to develop throughout the world a mass protest against war. And this is not all.

[37]

international affairs, claiming that the fault lies not with the machinery but with the human unwillingness to use it.

The *Federal Union Plan,* originated by Clarence K. Streit, began as *Union Now.* It advocates an immediate union of likeminded nations, pledged to the basic liberties, and leaving the latchstring out in the hope of serving as the nucleus for a world-government. The *Atlantic Union Plan* would restrict these charter members to the nations of the Atlantic Pact.

The Culbertson Plan, or ABC Plan, promoted by the *Citizens Committee for United Nations Reform,* proposes a drastic alteration of the United Nations Charter in order to get rid of the veto. Its proponents believe that such a change would be acceptable to the great powers if they were given a weighted representation in the Security Council. This plan would restrict the initial functions of the world agency to the prevention of war; and it contains detailed proposals for an effective world police force.

The *United World Federalists* (which absorbed *Americans United for World Government, World Federalists U. S. A.,* and other antecedent organizations) holds that nothing short of a world-government with adequate but limited powers will serve the purpose of preventing war. There would be a "vetoless" world legislature, with representation proportional to population, economic advancement and other factors; a smaller executive body; and a bill of rights. All armaments above the minimum needed for internal policing would be reserved for the world-government. The *World Constitution Plan* grew out of a radio address by Chancellor Hutchins, and was developed by a group drawn largely from the Faculty of the University of Chicago; it is the most radical plan of all in its departure from the United Nations, and in its advocacy of a world political organization with a detailed and elaborate constitution.

All thinking about world-organization has been affected, and to some extent overshadowed, by the growing rift between the Soviet Union, supported by its "satellites," and the United States, representing the so-called "free nations." In 1947, Walter Lippmann's book, *The Cold War,* gave currency to this name for the present unhappy phase of human history.*

The *cold war* describes a situation in which each party seeks to defeat the other by giving aid to the other's opponents, by economic measures, by propaganda, by preparations for war evidently aimed at the other party; in short, by any means short of the use and commitment of its armed forces. The so-called *Truman Doctrine,* formulated by the President

*Mr. Lippmann has informed me that the expression (*la guerre froid*) was widely used in France in the Thirties; and he would have preferred the other expression then current, namely, "the white war" (*la guerre blanche*), had it not been for the special meaning of "white" in the Russian context.

in his address to Congress on March 12, 1947, advocated aid to Greece and Turkey, and proposed to "aid free people to maintain free institutions against aggressive movements that seek to impose upon them totalitarian regimes." This was taken to mean that Communism and its spread throughout the world was regarded as the supreme danger against which the United States proposed to guard itself and its friends. Circumstances have combined to make this intent less clear. The Russian Menace has come to be viewed from a political, rather than an ideological, point of view; thus, the United States has found it desirable to encourage nationalistic Communism in Jugoslavia and elsewhere. At the same time, the attempt to stop Communism *everywhere* has appeared to be too vast an undertaking.

The *Marshall Plan*, otherwise known as the Economic Recovery Program (E. R. P.) and the Economic Coöperation Administration (E. C. A.), marked a shift of emphasis: Communism was to be not so much defeated or contained as averted in those parts of the world (such as Western Europe) where it was not yet established. It was conceived that the best way of achieving this end was to eradicate the seed-bed of Communism; namely, poverty, misery, disorder and unrest. In order to give economic aid to Western Europe, it was necessary to encourage strong ties between the European states themselves and between Europe and the Western

Hemisphere. The *North Atlantic Pact* (1949) was the logical sequel.

This Pact, like the Act of Chapultepec entered into by the American Republics in 1945, was based on Article 51 of the United Nations Charter, which provided for regional "collective self-defense." It was implemented by the *North Atlantic Treaty Organization*, the *Mutual Defense Assistance Program*, and finally by the appointment of General Eisenhower as Supreme Commander of the North Atlantic Treaty forces. The developments indicated a shift from the bolder Truman Doctrine toward defensive military measures—designed, to use General Marshall's words, "to curb Communist aggression and, if possible, to avoid another world war in doing so." [14]

With less emphasis, and on a much smaller scale, the United States has embarked on "a bold new program for making the benefits of our scientific advances and industrial progress available for the improvement and growth of underdeveloped areas." [15] This is commonly known as the *Point Four* program. It belongs to a phase of policy, known as *world development*, which will be considered in a later chapter.

The greater urgency of international problems, and the fact that the defense program now dominates the American economy, has brought about a temporary eclipse of the shibboleths used in the era of the New Deal and its aftermath. But they are still uttered, however faintly, from force of habit.

Free enterprise is still the favorite name for the doctrine favored by conservatives in the area of domestic policy. "Free" and "enterprise" are good words to the American ear, and the combination of the two is well-nigh irresistible. Strictly speaking, free enterprise means the freedom of business from interference by government—freedom to engage as one will in any form of production or marketing activity. This is an obsolete idea if it is taken to exclude *regulation* by government. And "free enterprise" does not meet the issue squarely insofar as it ignores such restrictions on enterprise or employment as result from monopoly or capitalistic exploitation.

The fact that the free enterprisers are in opposition has given a negative meaning to such terms as *collectivism* and *planned economy.* The former suggests socialism; the latter is a bad name because it stands for the proposal that government shall restrict individual initiative and the motive of private profit in the interest of a total or long-range view. It is charged that this subordination of the part to the whole results in *regimentation;* that is, organization at the cost of diversity and spontaneity. When used as a slogan, this charge takes no account of the regimentations which result from poverty or lack of opportunity.

The welfare state is an expression used by those

who feel that a system of social security weakens the will and capacity of individuals to look out for themselves. But it has not proved an effective weapon in party politics because, in the first place, no party proposes to withdraw the benefits of social security once they have been promised or enjoyed; and because in the second place, it is neither theoretically admissible nor popularly acceptable to deny that the state exists for the welfare of its people.

The term *politician* has a strong overtone of dispraise in American life. Many respected persons *are* politicians, but very few are willing to be *called* "politicians." It is the name which politicians are peculiarly fond of calling rival politicians—a notable instance of the pot-kettle argument. By definition, the politician is one versed in the science of government; but the disputes between the branches of the Federal Government, the jockeying for partisan advantage, and the fact that everybody in public life (the judiciary excepted) is a perpetual candidate, focus the "politician's" attention on getting elected to an office rather than on the performance of its duties. Even "going into politics" is considered a somewhat shady career. The lack of a *good* name for this essential human activity is regrettable. The term "statesman" is too pretentious—though there is force in the remark that "a statesman is a dead politician."

Labor relations, like everything else in America, tend to be dramatized. Hence the distortion of the term *collective bargaining*. Its good meaning is agreement reached by a discussion in which each party moderates its demands through understanding the point of view of the other. Collective bargaining in this sense does take place—privately and usefully. But the more common idea is that it is a conflict in which each party seeks to overcome the other by threats and by appeal to the gallery.

At the present time the hottest questions in domestic politics are those which reflect differences on questions of foreign policy. The idea of a *bipartisan* foreign policy, which prevailed for a short time owing largely to the prestige of the late Senator Vandenberg, does not suit the climate of American political life, except in time of actual war. As distinguished from "non-partisanship" it means that the two leading parties shall combine; but inasmuch as the primary object of an American party is to discredit and defeat the other party, two parties are not likely to be less partisan than one party—especially as election-day approaches.*

*A further difficulty arises from the fact that the Administration belongs to one of the two parties, and is likely to be too preoccupied with its administrative business for joint consultation. According to James Reston, one of the misconceptions in Washington was the idea that "the way to make the bipartisan foreign policy work is for the Secretary of State to tell Senator Vandenberg what he's going to do a few hours before he does it." *New York Times*, January 7, 1951.

[44]

Isolationism and *anti-isolationism* are no longer words to conjure by. There is, to be sure, an effect of remoteness in the central parts of the United States, but as of 1951 there are very few Americans who believe that America can afford to be indifferent to what goes on in the rest of the world. World-wide interdependence is now a condition and not a theory. In recent months, furthermore, it has been discovered that much of what has been called "isolationism" does not mean isolation in general, but isolation from some particular part of the world to which the isolationists have a peculiar antipathy: Europe may be emotionally much more alien than, let us say, Formosa.

Most highly charged of all are the words applied to those who are suspected of being friendly to the cold enemies; namely, Communism and Soviet Russia. The word *subversion* is the most deadly verbal weapon employed by Dies Committees and similar inquisitional groups, federal and state. The nearest approach to an official meaning of this term appears in the report of the Kerr Committee, a sub-committee of the House Appropriations Committee. It was afterwards cited by Mr. Justice Black in the case of *United States v. Lovett*, 1946:

Subversive activity in this country derives from conduct intentionally destructive of or inimical to the Government of the United States—that which seeks to undermine its institutions, or to distort its functions, or to impede its projects, or to overturn it all. Such activity may be open and direct as by effort to overthrow, or subtle and indirect as by sabotage.

Although this definition served as the ground on which the salaries of Robert Morse Lovett, Goodwin B. Watson and William E. Dodd, Jr. were withheld, President Roosevelt, when signing the bill, stated that he regarded this provision as unconstitutional. In a recent decision (April 30, 1951), the Supreme Court struck the names of three organizations designated as Communistic from the Attorney General's list of "subversive groups," on the ground that these groups had been denied proper hearings to prove themselves non-Communistic and to test the constitutionality of the Government's loyalty program.

The evil of the word "subversion" lies not only in the extreme vagueness of the idea itself, since it refers to the "intention" or "ultimate end" of the activity condemned, but in the fact that it has been taken to mean that it is a legal crime to be "subversive." It is popularly confused with sedition and treason. At most, subversion has to do with the screening of persons employed in departments or agencies of government; but it has become a highly injurious label applied promiscuously to persons of a relatively radical persuasion. One thing seems now to be established, namely, that the Attorney General cannot make people or groups illegally subversive by merely, like the Lord High Executioner, "putting them on his list."

[46]

During the period of coöperation between Communist and other parties of the Left in Europe, it was customary to speak of the "Popular Front," as in the case of the ministries of Léon Blum in France in 1936-38. This was perhaps the origin of the political use of the term "front" as the name for a coalition of groups holding similar ideas. The current meaning of the word "front" is something quite different. It has become a verbal weapon used to discredit a mixed group by *naming* it after its most objectionable member. "Give a dog a bad name and hang him"; or give a man a drop of mixed blood, and he becomes "colored" to white supremacists, or "Jewish" to professional Aryans. Thus, in America today, *Communist front* does not mean an association of different Communist groups and splinters, but an association of Communist and non-Communist groups, named accusingly for its Communist element, however small.

Applied retrospectively, this would mean that the Allies were a Communist front in the last war; and will become so again if they are joined by Jugoslavia. The Huks in Luzon include Communists, the resistance group of the Japanese occupation, and land-hungry peasants; but they are all *called* Communists.*

---

*A "Communist-dominated front" would be something different, but this distinction does not receive much attention, perhaps owing to the assumption that Communists always dominate any group to which they belong.

The expressions *fellow-traveller* and *guilt by association* suggest the indefinite enlargement of this alleged Communist contamination. There is a useful meaning of the first of these expressions, if applied to those who have become inveterate apologists for the Communist or Russian point of view as a result of trying to understand it and give it a fair hearing. There is an insidious corruption of the mind by which one leaps from an initial one-sidedness to an opposite one-sidedness.

There is also a fellow-travelling which means nothing but partial agreement: as when, let us say, Americans agree with Communists that "peace is a good thing." If such fellow-travelling is to be consistently avoided, one must reject a belief solely on the ground that an opponent holds it—a procedure strange, but not unknown. Partial agreement is not only inevitable but desirable, since it provides the only point of departure for the peaceful settlement of conflict.

Guilt by association, when loosely affirmed, is based on the unfortunate proverb that "a man is known by the company he keeps"; this axiom is peculiarly inappropriate to America, a country of mixed population, and the very life-blood of whose political life is discussion. Those who deny guilt by association protest against holding a person guilty because he is a member of an organized group which is held guilty as a whole. There is a double room for doubt here. The organization may or may not be guilty; if the organization is guilty the member may or may not share its guilt. The first doubt raises such questions as "subversion"; the second doubt raises the question of conspiracy. In times of excitement, the public mind is not seriously troubled by either doubt.

The broad effect of all three of these expressions—*front, fellow-traveller,* and *guilt by association*—is to polarize popular opinion. They discourage, and may destroy, that thoughtful discrimination which recognizes the complexities of an issue; they discourage, and may destroy, those groups in which men of different opinions meet, and in a temper of moderation learn from one another.

Cold war, like actual war, brings into play the charges of *pacifism* and *peace at any price,* together with the counter charge of *militarism.* All of these expressions confuse the popular mind by identifying an idea which is good in a limited sense with an idea which is bad in an extreme or doctrinaire sense. If *pacifism* meant only love of peace and giving peace a high rank in the order of human purposes, very few would object to being called a pacifist. The pacifist is of dubious repute when he is supposed to mean that there should never be a resort to violence, even in the extremity of self-defense.

Marshal Tito is quoted as saying that "humanity has had terrible experience with the policy of *peace at any price.*" He said that if one paid too much for

[49]

peace one did not get it, but only "a temporary respite." [16] Others using this expression mean that there is a limit to the price to be paid for peace; namely, the sacrifice of principle, or of those values which make peace worth having. The danger does not lie in condemning too high a price for peace, but in condemning, as though it were the same thing, the paying of *any* price whatever.

Militarism is, strictly speaking, the name for love of war for its own sake, or for the sake of power—a passion which is supposed to afflict the professional soldier or the ambitious ruler. It is applicable to a people who have become "trigger happy" as a result of the exciting of their combative emotions. But the term is often used by the party of peace as a term with which to discredit any preparation for war or form of military morale and discipline.

The terms (ordinarily of dispraise) applied to the enemy in the cold war can be roughly classified as ideological and political. *Communism* itself, needless to say, is now so abusive a term as to be libelous. Beyond this emotional meaning, it has many objective meanings. Taken as *socialism*, it means the ownership and direction, by society as a whole and for the benefit of society as a whole, of the means of production—as opposed to the capitalistic system of private ownership and profit. While the line cannot be sharply drawn, Communism is distinguished from socialism through emphasis on specifically Marxist doctrines, such as *historical determinism, class struggle, dialectical materialism* and *the proletarian revolution.*

Marxism descends from two sources in German philosophy, Hegel, and the materialist school represented by Feuerbach. Its Hegelianism consists in the doctrine that the historical process moves inevitably along a predetermined line, governed by a strife of ideas represented by opposing states or societies. Communism's materialism lies in the doctrine that these opposing ideas are *economic* ideas, represented by opposing economic classes; or more specifically, by the proletarian class of peasants and workers, and the bourgeois class of private property owners, merchants, professionals, and intelligentsia. The conflict is held to be inescapable, deadly, and destined to result, through revolutionary violence, in the victory of the proletariat. This ultimate *end*, of which the Communist regards himself as the chosen instrument, is held to justify any *means* by which it may be promoted.

The enemies of Communism may oppose it on any or all of the above points. Taken as a form of socialism, it is opposed by advocates of capitalism. Taken as determinism, it is opposed by those who believe in individual and creative historical causes. Taken as a gospel of struggle and violence, it is opposed by the friends of gradualism and peaceful per-

[51]

suasion. Taken as materialism, it is opposed by the friends of religion and the "higher spiritual values." Taken as justifying the means by the end, it is opposed, in the name of "morality," by those who accept certain moral precepts as absolute, or who insist that there is a higher end, and hence a higher justification, than that offered by Communism.

In recent years and in the light of the development of Communism under Stalin, the emphasis has shifted to its political meanings. Although Communism professes to believe in the withering away of the state, the *dictatorship* of the proletariat seems to have come to stay, and to have become indistinguishable from the oppressive tyrannies which have been the historic enemies of democracy. Its rulers, having come into power as leaders of revolution, seem to be primarily concerned with holding and increasing their power. The system of secret police, excused as a protection against counter-revolution, now appears as an instrument of intimidation. In keeping with an original Marxian doctrine that all of human culture should express and reinforce a central creed, the dictatorship, operating through its secret police, has extended its control not only to politics and economics, but to art, science and religion—until it appears that no deviation from a common orthodoxy is tolerated in word or deed.

These internal aspects of Communism give meaning to the expressions *police state, totalitarianism* and

relativism. Because of its resemblance in these respects, it has been easy to shift to Communism the
hostility so recently felt toward Fascism and Nazism.
Communists, on the other hand, since they care less
about the suppression of individual and cultural
freedoms, and more about who it is that does the
suppressing, can conceive of Fascism and Nazism as
signifying the ascendancy of industrial magnates and
landed proprietors, and therefore as Enemy No. 1.

It has always been a part of Communism's creed
that it would eventually conquer the world, and the
Comintern and the Cominform have been instruments designed to speed that conquest. But the term
imperialism did not come into use among our verbal
weapons of attack until this conquest came to assume
a more and more political character; until, in other
words, there appeared to be a design to bring large
areas of the world, outside of the old frontiers of
Russia, under the dictatorship of the Kremlin. Russian Communism has been enabled thus far to present
itself to the world as *anti-imperialism,* since it has
been directed against the historic European empires,
and has supported the widespread revolt against
European colonialism. Soviet Russia has been able,
by promoting Communist parties in other countries,
to expand without direct armed invasion; and, by
satisfying existing grievances, to give this expansion
the better name of "liberation"—not without some
degree of plausibility.

Having first associated it with lies, big and small, after the manner of Hitler and Goebbels, we have now come to recognize *propaganda* as a proper instrument of our own foreign policy. We have come back, in short, to the original and innocent meaning of the word as the organized propagation of doctrine. Or we distinguish honest propaganda from the technique of implanting in people's minds false beliefs which it is useful to us that they should hold. From long experience in the art of advertising, we should be experts in both kinds of propaganda.

What do we have, honestly speaking, to say for ourselves? For one thing, we call ourselves a *young country*. This is said out of mixed motives: as a confession of fault, as a promise of greater things to come, and as presenting an aspect of glamour. There is always the question of how long an individual or a country can continue to use youth as a boast, an alibi or a charm. It is true that as a state we were born as recently as 1776, but our people were not born then, or even our nation. And our political constitution is said to be the oldest on earth. So if we err, we have, after all, had time to learn better.

Democracy! Here we are confronted by the significant fact that both adversaries in the cold war claim the word. And whichever side wins, the victory will be celebrated in the *name* of "democracy." There is, then, our democracy and theirs—"the people's democracy," and "Western democracy." It is natural for us to assume that ours is the "real" or "true" democracy, and to scorn their use of the word. But it is not quite so simple as that. Historically speaking, one of the things that democracy has meant is the rise of the masses against the classes—the inverting of the social pyramid. If the term "masses" is equated with the workers and peasants, and the term "classes" with the bourgeoisie, then the Communist movement has, *in that respect,* been a democratic revolution. And if in that same respect *we* are to claim democracy, it is because we stand for the rise of the underprivileged to a higher level of well-being.

When, however, democracy is conceived in terms of *freedom,* the verdict must be very different. There is much more to be said on this topic—there are many freedoms. But it is clear that for us democracy is a set of freedoms—the freedom to think, communicate, criticize, and discuss; the freedom of art and science to follow their own bent; the freedom of persons to lead their own lives and develop in their own ways; the freedom of people to live under a government of their own choosing. The *civil liberties* which we are accustomed to emphasize consist of those essential liberties which, because they are essential to government of, for, and by the people, are deemed to be the condition of all other liberties.

The *free world,* which is the over-all name we now give to our side as opposed to the Communist world, is not made up exclusively of states and societies which enjoy the above freedoms. We include in "our side" notorious examples of the opposite. Nor can we say that the free nations of Western Europe, North America, and the British Commonwealth have fully achieved the freedom which they profess. So, to be accurate and properly humble, we must say that the free world consists of those nations which aspire to freedom, and in some degree realize it, together with such other nations as follow their lead.

CHAPTER IV

OUR MANY FREEDOMS

This chapter might have been entitled "The Land of the Free and the Home of the Brave," signifying that we are brave in the defense of freedom. But if this slogan is to be seriously affirmed and not merely sung, we are bound to ask ourselves what freedom means, or what *we* mean by freedom, or, better still, what we *propose* to mean by freedom.

It can be taken to mean a great many things. One meaning, happily, can be omitted. We are not concerned here with what is called "freedom of the will" —we can leave that to the metaphysicians. We are concerned rather with the question of freedom or liberty as it arises in connection with man's political and other social relations. And one may say "freedom *or* liberty" since, in the political and social field these words are used interchangeably.

Within this restricted field, the multitude of meanings is suggested by the different prepositions—"of," "from," and "for"—with which the word freedom is used. There is the freedom "of" science, art, and religion, and of the human person who possesses and enjoys the freedom. The list of freedoms so classified is as long as the list of human institutions and activities. But this distinction is by no means trivial. The whole meaning of the argument often turns on *whose* freedom is at stake. The profound difference between "my" freedom and "yours" or "theirs" is self-evident: what a man means when he claims freedom is usually "his" freedom.

The difference between "freedom from" and "freedom for" or "to" throws light on the root-meaning of the term. There is negative freedom and there is positive freedom. The former consists in the absence of restraint. When a man's jail sentence expires, he is free from bodily hindrance: he *may* now go where he likes. But *can* he? Not if he is bedridden. Not if he has nowhere to go. Not if the place where he would like to go is beyond his reach. So there is a positive freedom, not covered by "nobody is stopping you," which requires capacity. A man who at the time of retirement is freed from office routine cannot be said to be free to travel, or read good books, or listen to fine music, unless he "has what it takes." Positive freedom has to be implemented.

It would appear, then, that freedom in the full sense consists in *doing what one chooses because one so chooses*. This statement cannot be shortened without omitting something essential. There must be doing, and not merely wishing. There must be choos-

[58]

ing: not merely acting or desiring. And the doing must follow from the choosing. A lady of my acquaintance entered a hotel elevator, and while she was still in doubt as to whether she would or would not go up to her room, the elevator ascended; whereupon she said "I've decided." Freedom is not merely agreement between choosing and doing; it all depends on which is cause and which is effect.

A little history is now in order. Professor Whitehead once remarked in my presence that America had had "no eighteenth century," which was a startling observation because the United States of America was born in that century, and had appealed to the ideas of the eighteenth century in demanding its independence. His remark was an ironical way of saying that America took the ideas of the eighteenth century seriously, and exhibited none of that levity which characterized the England of the Georges. Whether this is true or not (and it is to be noted that Benjamin Franklin had his lighter side), Professor Whitehead might equally well have said that *only* America had had an eighteenth century.

We are here concerned not with the manners and morals of the eighteenth century but with those ideas which have given it the name of "The Enlightenment" or "The Age of Reason," and of which John Locke was the most conspicuous exponent. The central idea was that man was a "rational being," and that his problems, and his social problems in particular, could be solved by reason. This trust in reason was a reaction against authority, revelation, obscurantism, mysticism and mystification, inspiration, speculation, imagination and feeling—all conceived as hindrances to reason. Stated positively, the Enlightenment stood for clear ideas; and for the belief that reasons can be found for human institutions, so that men may accept them not blindly, or on faith, or on somebody's say-so, but with their eyes open, and in the light of day.

At the time of the Revolution, this wind of opinion blew strongly in America as well as in Europe. Through Thomas Jefferson, it found classic expression in the *Declaration of Independence,* America's perpetual Charter; and it was translated into political action by the *War for Independence.* Conceiving man as a being capable of governing his political behavior by deliberate choice, it defined the rôle of citizenship in American democracy.

Now let us turn to our more special topic of liberty, which, in the doctrine of the Enlightenment, was held to be an inalienable natural "right." It was a "right" because, since liberties tend to collide with one another, they can be enjoyed only when they are limited. A man's "right" is, then, the sphere assigned to him within a system of liberties.

Why was liberty called a "natural" right? The word "natural" did not mean what it means today in the expression "natural science"; it did not mean "physical." It did mean "original," but only because

it was believed that the original state of man, before
civil institutions were needed to make him behave,
was an ideal state. Moreover, the natural right was
essentially ideal, and only accidentally original; therefore, it was not necessary to abandon the idea when
men's views of history changed, and the reign of
the tooth and the claw took the place of the Garden
of Eden.

The natural right of liberty was thus what ought
to be, or what would be if men were reasonable. The
legal right enforced the natural right, but the natural
right was already *there,* in the ideal order testified to
by conscience. There was always an appeal, therefore, from legal to natural rights, for the purpose of
amending the former, and for the purpose of giving
recognition to rights hitherto neglected.

There were, and are, several kinds of arguments
for natural or ideal rights such as liberty. There is the
metaphysical or religious argument, which contends
that man was created free—that the world was so
constituted, or, at any rate, was intended to be so
constituted. Christian philosophers, and especially
Roman Catholic philosophers, are likely to hold that
man would have no natural rights at all were it not
for God. In other words, no God, no rights, and no
Declaration of Independence. But it would seem that
atheists also should hold to natural rights; and that
many theists would reverse the order, and say
that God, like civil institutions, only recognizes and

enforces rights which are valid independently of Him —which can then be said to be to His moral credit.

A second argument for the right of liberty is humanistic. It is said that each individual is equipped with a mind and is thus qualified to govern his own affairs. Liberty is a condition for which he is evidently designed, or, at least, fit. Thus Lincoln, who was a pious subscriber to the Declaration of Independence, argued for free labor against slave labor as follows:

As the author of man makes every individual with one head and one pair of hands, it was probably intended that heads and hands should coöperate as friends, and that that particular head should direct and control that pair of hands. As each man has one mouth to be fed, and one pair of hands to furnish food, it was probably intended that that particular pair of hands should feed that particular mouth—that each head is the natural guardian, director, and protector of the hands and mouth inseparably connected with it.[1]

A third argument, echoed in the Declaration, held the right of liberty to be a "self-evident truth." This argument has lost force in more recent times. Self-evidence has become suspect. Our knowledge of the way beliefs are acquired has led to the view that self-evidence is usually an effect of habit and custom: things *seem* self-evident whenever they are generally accepted.

Meanwhile there has been another argument—more

durable and of more universal appeal. The right of liberty, like that of life, is conceived in terms of the pursuit of happiness. A system of liberties gives to each individual the maximum opportunity to act upon his interests without interference; and it gives him a sense of security, since so long as he remains within bounds he need not fear interference, and so need not divert his energies to self-defense. Since a system of liberties confers these benefits on all, rather than on any one or a few at the expense of the rest, it may properly claim to be the highest moral good.

The maxim of *tolerance* touches the matter of individual liberty at many points. Historically it developed, at least in modern times, and notably in England and the Netherlands, out of the religious conflicts attending and growing out of the Protestant Reformation. In the seventeenth century, its great English and American advocates were Milton, William Penn, and Roger Williams. At the close of that century, John Locke wrote his famous *Letters Concerning Toleration.* Thomas Jefferson became its most eloquent champion in America, and largely through his influence it established itself as part of the basic American creed.

The principle of toleration was defended, first, as a means of preventing civil discord. It led to a definition of the relation of church and state, according to which the state should be benevolently neutral in religious matters: neither prohibiting any religious sect, nor promoting one at the expense of others. This implied that the state itself could be erected on secular principles, without presupposing any religious dogma or any form of worship.

At the same time, it was argued that toleration was a condition of attaining truth. Let me quote from what Locke said of religious toleration in one of his famous *Letters:*

True and saving religion consists in the inward persuasion of the mind, without which nothing can be acceptable to God. And such is the nature of the understanding that it cannot be compelled to the belief of anything by outward force. . . . It may indeed be alleged that the magistrate may make use of arguments. . . . But it is one thing to persuade, another to command; one thing to press with arguments, another with penalties. . . . For laws are of no force at all without penalties, and penalties in this case are absolutely impertinent; because they are not proper to convince the mind. . . . It is only light and evidence that can work a change in men's opinions; and that light can in no manner proceed from corporal sufferings, or any other outward penalties.

Here is Jefferson's restatement of the same doctrine:

Almighty God hath created the mind free, and manifested His supreme will that free it shall remain by making it altogether insusceptible of restraint. . . . All attempts to influence it by temporal punishments, or burthens, or by civil incapacitations, tend only to beget habits of hypocrisy and meanness.[2]

[64]

In other words, force does not convince, but can only induce outward conformity. True conviction is reasoned conviction—that is, belief founded on the appropriate evidence; and if men are to be thus convinced they must be provided with the evidence, and be left free to follow it.

Both Locke and Jefferson saw the broader implications of this doctrine. Government by consent and public education follow from the idea that men should be permitted and enabled to think for themselves. The same idea applies not only to religious and political opinion, but to scientific and economic opinion as well.

It is to be noted that this doctrine was not the doctrine of Justice Holmes, as that is commonly construed. It did not mean that opinions should be free in order to compete with one another in the "market place," the strongest to prevail, but in order to be accepted in the light of evidence. In short, the philosophers of the Enlightenment and the Founding Fathers of the American Republic believed that the truth is one and objective, and that it will capture men's minds if they are opened to it.

The American Revolution was a political revolution—a revolution against the yoke of an alien ruler. Furthermore, settlers in a virgin territory, of vast expanse and rich in natural resources, felt themselves both compelled and competent to get along with little government. It was natural, therefore, that the

[65]

idea of freedom most emphasized in the early days of our history should be freedom from government. And as American culture became more diversified, freedom from government came to mean not a general freedom of individuals to do as they pleased, but a freedom of special human activities, such as business enterprise, science, art, and religion, to pursue their own ends. Freedom was praised as an encouragement of invention, genius, and private organization, in all the different walks of life. The spectacle of totalitarianism abroad has led Americans to appreciate this freedom at home.

Even the frontiersman, however, discovered that order was necessary if men were to enjoy the fruits of their self-reliance and labor. There could be no safety of life or property without law and a power to enforce it. In other words, while there is a freedom *from* government there is also a freedom *under* government; that is, a freedom from private interference secured by public authority. Similarly, all the cultural freedoms were seen to require a legal and political system to protect them from one another.

There is a freedom from government, a freedom under government, and also a freedom *for* government. It is this last freedom on which attention is focussed at the present time. It embraces those freedoms which are essential to popular government: freedom to think for oneself and communicate one's thoughts to others, freedom to criticize the government in power, freedom to vote at the polls, and the freedom of such agencies as the press, radio, private organizations and assemblies, through which opinions are aired, exchanged and discussed. A government which suppresses these freedoms loses its rightful authority as a "free government," or government by consent.

These freedoms form the core of the so-called "civil liberties" and "bills of rights." Together with the rights of habeas corpus, inviolability of domicile and equality before the law, they represent those freedoms the violation of which by a democratic government would contradict the very purpose for which that government exists, and destroy its claim to obedience.

There is a grave and unavoidable difficulty which arises from the freedom of thought and expression. A political democracy is pledged to tolerate and protect these freedoms. But what if they are used for the purpose of undermining their own foundations? Ought a political democracy, in the name of freedom, to permit thought and expression which, if carried into practice, would prohibit freedom of thought and expression? Or ought it to deny freedom of thought and expression in order to preserve them?

The key terms in these questions are the terms "ought" and "if carried into practice." The "ought" refers to the fundamental creed of freedom; if there were no such creed there would be no problem. The creed is the premise on which the question is argued. The problem is not escaped by legislation making the exercise of freedom illegal; the real question is not "should such a law be obeyed?" but "should there be such a law?" "If carried into practice" means that there is a crucial difference between the thought and the deed. A government pledged to the creed of freedom must prevent the destruction of freedom, but it does not follow that it must prevent the harboring and communicating of destructive ideas. Homicide is forbidden and punished, but not the entertaining of homicidal ideas unless they are executed in acts or threats. Similarly, it is possible to disbelieve in freedom without killing it or even wounding or threatening it.

The question becomes acute in proportion as the interval between the thought and the deed, or the idea and the effect, is diminished; and in times of public agitation, or owing to skilful propaganda, the interval may be very narrow. There is no *simple* rule which applies to concrete cases, because every concrete case is a *situation* involving a unique set of circumstances. This is the reason for the famous test formulated by Justice Holmes:

The character of every act depends upon the circumstances in which it is done. . . . The question in every case is whether the words used are used in such circumstances and are of such a nature as to create *a clear and present danger* that will bring about the substantive evils

[68]

that Congress has a right to prevent. It is a question of proximity and degree.[3]

Whether there is a clear and present danger must be left to the courts, which can take the circumstances into account: the solution, in other words, is found in a broad formula, implemented by broad precedents and wise judges. No better method has yet been proposed for dealing with the menace of revolutionary thought and expression.

This solution stands midway between two extremes, neither of which is a solution at all. A policy of *no* restriction of freedom of thought and expression means that a government pledged to support freedom denies itself the right to do so when freedom is in the gravest peril. It violates its own creed by inaction. On the other hand, a policy of unlimited restriction violates its democratic creed by too much action. For it is a part of its creed of freedom that the creed itself should be freely adopted.

For the creed of freedom is not a dogma, or a forced opinion, or an opinion held through ignorance, but a preferred belief chosen in the light of opposing alternatives. And these alternatives are not likely to be known and given their due weight unless they are voiced and advocated with some degree of conviction. The possibility of error and false belief is the price of truth. The possibility of incitement to subversive action is the price paid for a loyalty based on persuasion.

[69]

Emphasis on the political freedoms has led Americans to under-emphasize those other freedoms for the loss of which government is not responsible. If there were no government to deprive men of freedom, it would still be threatened, diminished, or destroyed by other causes. In their resentment of the excesses of government, men forget the enemies of freedom from which they have been saved by government. These other enemies are more original, more pervasive, and more persistent than government. In a well-governed society men can, and often do, pass their lives without ever feeling themselves restricted by government.

Lincoln's observations have a peculiar capacity to stand the test of time, as when he said:

The shepherd drives the wolf from the sheep's throat, for which the sheep thanks the shepherd as his liberator, while the wolf denounces him for the same act as the destroyer of liberty, especially as the sheep was a black one. Plainly, the sheep and the wolf are not agreed upon a definition of the word 'liberty'; and precisely the same difference prevails to-day, among us human creatures . . . all professing to love liberty.[4]

In other words there is a conflict of freedoms, and men accept the loss of one to gain another which they value more. Certainly in a democratic society the yoke of government is light as compared with those of incapacity, poverty, ignorance, economic dependence, and mass opinion.

When freedom is defined as *doing what one chooses because one so chooses,* then incapacity is one of its enemies. Sickness is an enemy of freedom. The boasted freedom of the Stoic to defy the handicaps of sickness depended on his possessing unimpaired the faculty of reason. The greatest enemies of freedom, which still defeat it throughout the greater part of mankind, are poverty and ignorance. The poor man lacks the means to do what he chooses. His lack of means keeps him at the level of bare subsistence and anchors him to his livelihood. He has "no other alternative." Long hours of hard labor leave him little time or strength either to choose or to do what he chooses.

Ignorance deprives men of freedom because they do not know what alternatives there are. It is impossible to choose to do what one has never "heard of." People choose more freely as they do today in the hitherto dependent areas of the world and in the hitherto unprivileged sections of society, because they have learned of new possibilities. Owing to the development of world-wide communication, "the news has got around." Authorities of church or state who wish to keep their people in subservience have long recognized the importance of keeping them in ignorance.

Among the social threats to freedom is to be numbered the parent, and in particular the father. Though domestic tyranny is now considerably reduced in power in the Western world, perhaps the celebration of its fall is premature. Another and greater potential enemy of freedom is the employer; or, rather, the economic system of which the employer is the more or less innocent instrument. It is one of the boasts of the capitalistic society that labor is mobile, so that a man may choose his livelihood. This is true *comparatively:* as compared, for example, with the stagnant condition of an old-world peasantry, or the enforced labor of a totalitarian society. The possibility, even though it is often merely a theoretical possibility, that a man may labor how and where he chooses is an essential ingredient of American life, and an exciting prospect to immigrants from abroad.

But this must not blind us to the fact that in the majority of cases this possibility is not realized. "The rising man" is not a myth, but neither is it a description of the common lot. There are many stagnant areas, both industrial and rural, in which each new generation finds itself committed to the occupation of the last; and this despite the opportunities afforded by the public education, and despite the fact that Americans are now aware of these obstacles to freedom and are by way of removing them.

A major enemy of freedom is the pressure of mass opinion and sentiment. If freedom is choice, whatever stands in the way of the individual's thinking and deciding for himself stands in the way of his freedom. The development of mass communication, and the failure of education, expose the mind of thinking citizens to the well-nigh overwhelming force of the currents and tides of opinion that ebb and flow about them. Here is a new subserviency, and consequently, a new freedom to be won and safeguarded, if democracy is to fulfill its promise.

The American idea of individual liberty can be stated in terms of those opposites of liberty which find American soil uncongenial. Thus, the American idea of individual liberty is opposed to authoritarianism. It accepts no authority as final because authority must justify itself to the reason of those who live under it; otherwise there is no obligation to obey. The American idea of individual liberty is opposed to paternalism—which is less clear, but no less certain. Paternalism is the most insidious form of authoritarianism, because it professes benevolent intentions. It is named for the father, who "knows what is best." The American idea of liberty, on the other hand, assumes that each individual knows his own interest, and is its only authentic spokesman. The American, infused with this idea, is not prepared to accept what others think is "good for" him; nor does he feel gratitude for favors conferred, but prefers to achieve good things for himself. The American idea of individual liberty is opposed to totalitarianism, the doctrine, namely, that individuals exist for the sake of some greater whole—such as the state, or the nation, or the race.

[73]

Unmistakably, and in the true spirit of the Enlightenment, the American idea of individual liberty is opposed to what is called the "positivistic" doctrine of human institutions; the doctrine, namely, that the legal, political, or economic system *as it stands* is on that account deserving of acceptance. History, tradition and the established order of things are open to criticism, and enjoy a title to acceptance only insofar as they earn such acceptance. All along the line, there is an appeal from the "is" to the "ought to be." Institutions are acceptable only insofar as they prove themselves to the individuals who live under them. Only insofar as this is the case, is it reasonable for men to accept them; only insofar as this is the case do men obey them, not from habit, coercion, or prestige, but from their own free choice.

The ultimate value of freedom lies in what is done with it. If freedom is to be given full dignity, it must include some worthy activity, of which freedom provides the condition. Freedom from obstacles, and freedom to do what one chooses, may be empty or trivial. A free family or circle of friends, without love, becomes "as sounding brass, or a tinkling cymbal." There is no boredom like that which can afflict people who are free, and nothing else. And boredom, in turn, may lead to fanaticism and violence. Finding nothing else to live for, a man may sacrifice himself blindly to a Cause. In losing himself, he feels no loss since his self is of no value. This is a strength of totalitarianism, and a danger to systems which give the individual freedom but fail to provide him with interests for which he values his freedom.

CHAPTER V

WHO TEACHES CITIZENSHIP?

That wise and responsible citizen of America and of the world, Benjamin Franklin, wrote to his friend Dupont de Nemours as follows:

We must not expect that a new government may be formed as a game of chess may be played, by a skilful hand, without a fault. The players of our game are so many, their ideas so different, their prejudices so strong and so various, and their particular interests, independent of the general, seeming so opposite, that not a move can be made that is not contested; the wisest agree to some unreasonable things, that reasonable ones of more consequence may be obtained; and thus chance has its share in many of the determinations, so that the play is like trictrac [backgammon] with a box of dice.[1]

Many years before, Franklin had written a letter to another friend, Cadwallader Colden, who wished to devote himself to science:

I wish you all the satisfaction that ease and retirement from publick business can possibly give you. But let not your love of philosophical amusements have more than its due weight with you. Had Newton been pilot but of a single common ship, the finest of his Discoveries would scarce have excused or atoned for his abandoning the Helm one hour in time of danger; how much less if she carried the fate of the Commonwealth.[2]

Americans are fortunate in numbering Benjamin Franklin among their ancestors. He understood the difficulties of statecraft, and he knew from his own experience that the goal of political action cannot be reached as the crow flies, but only by following the terrain, with such ups and downs, pauses and detours, as its surface may require. He understood this, but did not on that account evade the responsibilities of citizenship. On the contrary, he accepted a duty proportional to the difficulty and gravity of the task.

Democracy is both the best and the most difficult form of political organization—the most difficult because it is the best. The child who shakes his playpen, throws out his toys and raises general havoc until he is released and allowed to risk his life abroad, does not have to be taught to seek freedom. Something of this temper persists throughout life, and it is the impulse that can be most surely relied on for the cult of freedom. But as life advances in complexity, so does freedom. Like everything else, it has to be organized, and requires not only a stubborn willfulness but patient contrivance.

There is an ancient maxim that "art is long"— longer than life—which suggests that equally familiar maxim that "eternal vigilance is the price of liberty." Political liberty is an art; it does not merely happen, by the grace of nature or God; nor can it be counted on to remain after it is painfully achieved. America has more than once been threatened with the loss of its liberties. Throughout most of its history this land has been a refuge for men denied liberty elsewhere: today there is a trickle, not as yet a current, in the reverse direction, of writers and artists who look elsewhere for freedom to pursue their vocations, being victims of persecution, official and unofficial, in America.*

Whether freedom continues to flourish and grow in America depends, like everything else in America, on the quality of its citizenship. This, in turn, depends on education. It is customary to associate "education" with formal or organized education; that is, with what goes on in schools, colleges, and universities. But if education is taken to mean the totality of the influences by which the minds and characters of Americans are molded, this formal education is only a small part of the story.

There is an education which proceeds unceasingly in school and out, before school, and after one's last graduation. When the child is first subjected to formal education, he is already educated. While he is being formally educated, he is at the same time being educated by his family, by his association with contemporaries of all ages, and by all the experiences

*This is true, for example, of Paul Draper, the dancer, and Larry Adler, the musician; cf. *New York Times*, April 23, 1951.

of nature and social environment which fall outside the curriculum. And after his education is supposed to be "completed," he continues to be educated by his vocation, by his friendships and neighborly contacts, by his recreations and travels, by his participation in the institutions of church and state, by his reading of books, magazines and newspapers, and by his exposure to radio, motion pictures, television, and theatre. He continues to be educated up to his death, which is his last and perhaps most poignant lesson, from which, in this world at least, he is given no opportunity of profiting.

There is an education *in* later life as well as an education *for* later life; and if education for later life is to be what it professes to be, its effects must not only persist, but must enable men to meet and profit by the educational influences to which they will later be subjected. There is good reason, therefore, why a survey of education for citizenship should begin with this adult period, for which what goes before is supposed to be a preparation.

It is an ironical and inescapable fact that while the non-formal education of later life is the larger part of education, speaking the last word, and never silent, it is governed by no educational purpose. The tardy and half-hearted efforts which are usually referred to as "adult education" are pitifully inadequate, and can be accounted as no more than symptoms of a remorseful conscience. The major forces which mould the individual in "after life" are designed for other purposes. Their educational influence is incidental, and their total impact upon the development of mind and character is as much beyond the individual's control as the climate and the weather. To describe them would be to make an inventory of human culture. But there is one set of these forces which, in view of its growing importance and its direct attack on the mind, merits special emphasis; namely, the agencies of publicity.

In recent years there has been a vast increase in the range and power of these agencies. Newspapers, weeklies, and monthly magazines have been multiplied both in number and in circulation; radio receivers and television sets are found in nearly every home; best sellers and books-of-the-month flood our shelves; the motion pictures are attended by millions and have largely superseded the theatre attended by thousands.

This development is sometimes considered to be in itself evidence of the progress of education; whereas it is, in itself, evidence only of the progress of communication; that is, of agencies which, *for better or for worse*, influence and mould the minds of men from the nursery to the grave. The catch is that "for better or for worse." It is true that the growth of communication argues a growth of literacy; that is, of the capacity to read, write, and look. The minds of more men, more of the time, have become more accessible through the eye and the ear—more vulner-

able to visual and auditory signs. Never was the eye
assailed or the ear bombarded by so many words and
pictures. But with what effect—there's the rub!

If by education is meant educational *values*—inheritance of tradition, historical perspective, contribution to the civilization of the future, respect for
true and certified knowledge, understanding of the
purposes of social institutions, refinement of taste,
love of perfection, and, above all, capacity for disinterested political judgment—if education means such
things as these, then there is no reason whatever to
suppose that more communication constitutes or implies more education. For if one were to make a list
of all the opposites, and call them educational dis-
values or maleducation, then mere communication itself would serve them equally well. And this is, in
some degree, precisely what it does.

The sobering fact is that the instruments of mass
communication do not operate under educational
controls. They can be used for true educational ends,
but they need not be. The subject matter of mass
communication is not decided upon by chance or
whim, nor are the motives which govern its choice,
to put it mildly, unmixed. In a land of "free enterprise," publicity is a free enterprise, which means
that it is one of the many ways in which private producers make their private fortunes. The effect, if not
altogether desirable, is at least logical. Publicity enterprises prosper in proportion to the size of their

[*81*]

public, and their concern, like that of other business enterprises, is to reach and satisfy the largest possible number of consumers who can pay the price. The producers therefore study and practice the arts of mass appeal and entertainment. The press and magazines are interested in circulation, the publisher in bestsellers, the radio in the program that will attract the most listeners, the cinema in films that will crowd the theatres, and television in whatever will appeal to every family circle, including the dozing grandparents, the tired parents, and the children who should be in bed.

In order to attract and hold the attention of the largest number of consumers, mass communication will be designed to appeal to men's inclinations and habits as they stand, and to their least common denominator. Its producers will practice the art of salesmanship; they will seek to excite a demand for the goods which they produce and, since they are interested in the volume of sales, they will therefore excite the sort of demand which is excitable on a large scale. They will appeal to what is primitive and rudimentary in human nature rather than to that which is developed; to what is easy rather than to what is hard; to what is emotional rather than to what is thoughtful. Insofar as it is governed by a merely commercial motive, mass communication debauches the public taste to which it panders. Like patent-medicines and chewing gums, which are of comparable nutritive value, it is packaged and trade-marked.

Mass communication thus exploits and promotes what a recent writer has referred to as "commercialized semi-literacy." [3] It lends itself to the encouragement of that type of mind which is represented by the character of Tewler, in H.G. Wells' *You Can't be too Careful,* as described by a recent critic:

He is the passive, suggestible, mentally monocellular human being whose vast inane face is to be met with in all the Broadways and Main Streets of the world, the end-product of picture-magazines, bad education, mass entertainment, and a vulpine competitive society. [4]

The victims of such maleducation are in a sense less civilized than the peasants, craftsmen or tradesmen of an earlier age, who at least took their cue from an élite and their standards from tradition. "A higher standard of living" does not necessarily imply a higher standard of value. There may be more to choose from, but less assurance that the selection will be wise.

This picture is overdrawn, but its exaggeration is justified by its gravity. What is the remedy? There are three possibilities, no one of which can be wholly ignored. The first possibility is to reform the producers. There are notable producers of publicity who are governed by non-commercial motives, and who consider the beneficence, and not merely the sale, of their wares; perhaps there is no producer of books, newspapers, magazines, radio or television programs, or motion pictures who is not at times overtaken by a sense of educational responsibility, or ruled by canons of good taste, scholarly accuracy and artistic merit. These motives should be praised when they appear. The only complaint against magazines such as the *Atlantic Monthly* and *Harper's,* and weeklies such as the *New Yorker,* the *Nation,* the *New Republic* and *Commonweal,* is that they reach so limited a circle of readers.

Moreover, if America has the worst newspapers in the world, it also has the best—the *New York Times,* the *New York Herald Tribune,* the *Washington Post,* the *St. Louis Post-Dispatch,* the *Louisville Courier-Journal* and others in various parts of the country. Such newspapers acknowledge and perform a duty of public education. They are the greatest news-gatherers in human history; they are served by journalists who obey a professional code of scrupulousness and fairness, and who are skilled in the art of lucid exposition. If America has the worst column and editorial writers in the world, its best rank high. The same may be said of radio, magazines, popular books, and even the much-abused movies. Some of their productions are inflammatory, irresponsible, and debasing; others, and all honor to them! contribute notably to public enlightenment.*

*We should, I think, learn to number such men as E. B. White, James B. Reston, Walter Lippmann and Edward R. Murrow among the great *teachers* of the day.

If there is any fault to be found with the better agencies of publicity, it is a fault of their merit. In obedience to a code of fairness, they present "both sides of the question," and a program is called "educational" when the ring is open to all comers on equal terms.[5] This dramatization of conflicting opinions holds the interest of the audience or reader, and at the same time exonerates the manager from the charge of prejudice. But the effect is often to generate more heat than light, and scarcely helps the citizen to judge the question on its merits. In any case, the avowedly educational programs and printed pages are occasional departures—a small fraction of the total impact of organs of news and opinion. They serve to conciliate critics and salve the consciences of authors, but they appeal to a small and select constituency.

The press is not without its critics, among journalists themselves as well as among friends of the public. The United Nations Sub-commission on Freedom of the Press (Economic and Social Council), and in America, the Hutchins Commission on Freedom of the Press, the American Press Institute at Columbia, and the Nieman Fellowships in Journalism at Harvard have all emphasized the immense social responsibility of the press in the modern age. Thus, the Hutchins Commission described the obligation of the press to enable the people to make "fundamental de-

[85]

cisions necessary to the direction of their government and their lives." [6]

While highly laudable, these exceptional practices and exhortations to reform cannot be said to promise a solution of the problem. The good practices do not as yet reach the bulk of the people; the reforms are not as yet executed. The reason for the failure lies in the fact that the owners of newspaper and other agencies of mass communication are in business. The producer can be encouraged to set his house in order and raise his standards of public service; but in the last analysis the rewards of success and the risks of failure will operate as stronger incentives than his sense of public responsibility, and the recognized code of a competitive economy will enable him to appease his conscience.

The second possibility of reform is to place the agencies of publicity under the control of government. But this would create a vicious circle. Government rests on public opinion, and if public opinion is the product of the aimless impact of agencies of publicity, then the control by government will reflect this aimlessness. Or, assuming that government is governed by an educational purpose, it will create the very opinion on which it rests, which violates the maxim that authority originates with the people at large.

This is only a fraction of the difficulty. For a public control of the agencies which affect people's minds, a control which permitted the circulation only of such ideas, beliefs and emotional stimuli as government officials deemed educationally valuable, would kill that spirit of intellectual, imaginative, and artistic inventiveness which enriches civilization and creates that reservoir of cultural goods from which the best can be selected. That government should exercise *some* control—such as may be necessary to prevent libel, or offenses against decency, or threats to security—and that it should establish its own agencies of publicity designed to inform the public and to interpret its policy, is one thing; but it would be another and an abhorrent thing to have government regulate *all* agencies of publicity, to have it become a colossal pedagogue, board of censors, or Watch and Ward Society, treating the people as tenderminded wards who do not know what is good for them and must therefore be spoon-fed by their betters.

There remains a third possibility, which unfortunately would take time to bring results. This third possibility is to control the agencies of publicity, not directly through the reform of the producer or control by government, but indirectly, through the education of the consumer. When charged with lacking a sense of public responsibility, the producer passes the responsibility on to the customer, and claims that the people get what they want: this third possibility, then, is to accept this transfer of responsibil-

[87]

ity, and look to the character and quality of what people want.

It is quite true that the people get what they want. It is not true that individuals and select groups always get what they want; they are obliged to accept what a sufficient number of people want. To pay the costs of production, there must be a certain volume of demand; and it is this voluminous demand, rather than the demand of an élite, which determines the quality of the product. This trend to mass supply in response to mass demand is so in agreement with the economic forces of the day that it appears to be irreversible. Those who merely deplore it are wasting their time and nervous energy. A more fruitful approach to the problem, even though the fruit cannot be immediately harvested, is to raise the level of mass demand.

The chief merit of the free enterprise system is that it induces a few able men to invest in an effort to give a large number of other men what they want. Let us suppose the case of what would ordinarily be considered a "bad" newspaper. The proprietor lies awake nights devising means of giving his readers what they find interesting. They are not compelled to buy his newspaper, or to read it if they do buy it. They will not be likely to buy it if they do not read it. If they do not buy it, the circulation will drop, the advertisers will fall away and the newspaper will fail.

So the proprietor, more or less reluctantly assisted by his salaried staff, *tempts* his customers to read.

He knows the bait which will make them bite. If they like their news slanted or sensational, he slants it and sensationalizes it; he arrests their attention by glaring headlines, and feeds their love of excitement by supplying stimuli to their pet hates and their morbid curiosity. If they like comics, he gives them the comics they like. In his sporting page, he caters to the popular interest in competition and to the worship of athletic heroes, regardless of the effect on education and amateur standards. He employs columnists who are popular, regardless of what they think or say. Day in and day out he watches the response, whether it be in circulation figures or in letters to the editor. He stakes his private fortune and devotes his talents to discovering and providing what a considerable aggregate of men ask for and are willing to pay for.

But it is to be noted that he has no objection to doing his customers good if sufficient numbers of them want the good. "The customer is always right," even when he *is* right. It is one of the great merits of free enterprise that it is without malice. As an exercise of the imagination, let us suppose that the masses of mankind wanted to know the truth about nature and society, preferred good art to bad, and in matters of public policy wished to reach as wise a conclusion as possible amidst the conflict of interests and opinions. The agencies of publicity would then be compelled by their economic interest to cater to this higher demand, and to invent ways of satisfying it. Every rise in the level of demand would lead to an improvement of the product, and this in turn would confirm and raise the level of demand. The circle would then be benign and not vicious.

This, it will be objected, is a large supposition, and a supposition contrary to fact. But it defines a line of effort and indicates a place to break the existing vicious circle; namely, in the school, college, and university. Formal education is, as we say, a "non-profit making" enterprise. It owes allegiance to no end save the end of education. In forming the minds of the to-be-educated, it is not usurping any other social function, but is merely doing what it is designed to do; and though the immediate results may be small, they are cumulative, since each generation which is educated becomes an ally in the education of the generations which follow.

The remedy calls for a fresh orientation of formal education, beginning as early as the elementary schools. The individual would be taught how to swim in the great ocean of publicity in which he is presently to be immersed. He would learn how to keep his head above water while making headway, how to navigate the waters without being engulfed and drowned.

Metaphors aside, this would mean that the formal-

ly educated individual would be made acquainted
with what the agencies of mass communication *are*—
their dangers as well as their usefulness, their commercial motivations as well as their educational possibilities—all very concretely in terms of names and
places. He would have learned to discriminate and
choose amidst the welter of news and opinion. He
would have acquired sales resistance and yet know
how to buy, for his initial scepticism would nevertheless permit him to believe. He would, in short, be
the maker and guardian of his own mind.

If education in this sense is to operate as an effective control of publicity in an age of mass communication, it must be widely disseminated—widely
enough to determine the general mind of the book-
and-magazine reading, the radio listening, and the
motion picture and television listening and seeing,
public. Insofar as it was disseminated, it would greatly serve that ideal of democracy which requires that
the people at large shall be the qualified managers
of their own affairs and masters of their own destiny.

CHAPTER VI

THE ACADEMIC COMMUNITY
OF FREEDOM

Some years ago a young man of my acquaintance was compelled by straitened circumstances to leave college at the end of his freshman year and to embark somewhat prematurely on life "out in the world." In his late forties, after some years in journalism and business, he returned to college to resume his studies and he reported his impressions of the so-called "educated men" whom he had met. He said that he had found no difference between the university clubs and any other clubs—the same padded leather chairs, the same level of conversation (cards, baseball, golf), and the same resentment felt against anyone who introduced serious topics. He concluded that "it is comparatively easy to *get* educated; the difficult thing is to *stay* educated." He might have expressed a doubt as to whether a man who does not stay educated *is* educated.

Another young friend retired from the practice of law because he found that he was losing his mind; losing, that is, the capacity to read and think for him-

self, happily acquired during the period of his studies. Having been assigned the task of giving legal
advice to corporations, he found that he was coming
to be corporation-minded. His mind was being
formed by his clients and his legal associates.

It is not easy, then, even if the mind has been lib-
erated and stocked in youth, to keep it free in after
life. The intellectual impressions of college days are
not indelible, but are likely to fade into glamorous
reminiscences revived from time to time by class re-
unions. Education *for* later life is likely to be ex-
pelled and replaced by attitudes, habits and opinions
acquired *in* later life.

Nor is it clear just how the formally educated man
is expected to show it. One such judgment is illustrated by a conversation I once had in a broadcasting
studio while awaiting my time at the microphone.
The professional radio expert and I were listening to
a broadcast of the dedication of the Jefferson Memorial in Washington. President Roosevelt, who was to
dedicate the Memorial, was delayed, and the commentator was obliged to fill in the time. He rambled
on in the usual manner: "A vast throng is assembled.
There is blue sky overhead. It appears that the President is about to arrive. There he comes—no, not yet—
the crowd is growing impatient. There he is at the
door, and now he is coming down the aisle, accompanied by his staff," etc., etc. So I remarked: "It seems

to be important for men in your work to be able to keep on talking even when they have nothing to say." "Yes," he replied, "that's the reason why it is necessary in the radio business to have a college education."

This is not the educator's idea of his end product. A "Civic Education Project" is preparing series of pamphlets, so written as to be understood by pupils in secondary schools. The titles of the pamphlets already issued, *The Isms—and You, Who Says So?*, and *Why Don't They Think?*, indicate the emphasis on preparing young Americans to understand the issues of the day, and to play their part in the making of public opinion.[1] Attention should be called also to "Education for Citizenship," issued in 1940 by the New York Teachers Association. These are among the many signs that those responsible for secondary education in America are not satisfied with the present provision for the teaching of "civics." [2]

The faculties of colleges and universities participate in adult education, more or less reluctantly and unsuccessfully, through "popular" books and articles. They reach the thousands and not the millions. They are read by only a small fraction even of those who were once their students. This is a praiseworthy effort, but it does not meet the problem. The interest and the capacity to respond are not there.

In the curriculum of higher education, it is not

customary to offer courses on citizenship*—partly because it is thought to be unworthy of the "scholar," and partly because it is assumed that all courses teach citizenship. That there are few, if any, courses which are so described is not important. The condition of the graduate's mind is a better test than the catalogue. The fact that "college men" are so vulnerable to the mass opinion and sentiment of their time is evidence of failure. Thus, for example, no one can have lived through the recent wave of intolerance without meeting fellow-graduates who seem to have no inkling of the meaning of freedom of thought—who, despite their education, still think it means freedom for *their* thoughts, or for the thoughts of which *they* approve. If they once learned better, they have forgotten their lesson.

Those colleges and universities which select their students, and thus extend their advantages to a small fraction of the population, nevertheless consider themselves justified in asking for wide support, on the ground that they prepare the "leaders" in busi-

*A notable exception is the course on "Great Issues" offered at Dartmouth College. In this course (in 1950-1951) the students examined not only the issues, but the "mass media" of communication—newspapers, radio, etc. They were addressed by specialists in their fields, and compelled to think and discuss with special reference to the moral, social, and political values involved. The prospectus of this course contains admirable statements of the purpose which is here advocated. Similar courses are beginning to appear in other colleges.

ness, the arts and professions, and the government service. This they do. But these leaders are not necessarily leaders either in the understanding or in the practice of freedom. Furthermore, in a democracy leaders require followers, and even the most distinguished colleges and universities have the task of educating the far more numerous group of ordinary people who in the last analysis determine the kind of leadership which can effectively lead.

A program for teaching citizenship on the level of higher education would include a knowledge of the facts of life. The immense development of the social sciences, and the inclusion of such studies in the new programs of "general education," guarantees some acquaintance with social ideas and practices—political, economic, and psychological. As education for citizenship in later life, this is in itself not sufficient. In order that such knowledge is to be profited by in later life, a connection must be made at the time when it is acquired. It must be earmarked for use—otherwise when the time comes for its use it will not be recognized as relevant: it will belong to the past history of the mind and not to its present resourcefulness.

The extent to which the teachers of social science prepare their students for citizenship is further limited by their self-imposed code. As in other subjects, such as philosophy and literature, in which it is likewise respectable to entertain different opinions, teachers hesitate to teach their students how to choose among them, and hesitate themselves to choose.

But thought is applied to action through *decision*. Giving students ideas without enabling them to draw conclusions is like giving them sharpened tools without teaching them what to do with them. There are many fields of inquiry in which it is impossible to reach exact and certain results. As a matter of fact, it is impossible to reach exact or certain results in most of the important affairs of life. I might mention matrimony. It is not possible to reach a conclusion concerning the choice of a wife or husband that is comparable in exactness and certainty to the conclusions reached in mathematics, or physics, or indeed in any of those life sciences or social sciences most immediately concerned. No one, however, would on that account recommend that one should either remain unmarried, or go it blind. Furthermore, one cannot postpone the decision indefinitely. If one is to enjoy the benefits of marriage, one must decide within a limited time. The same may be said of one's choice of a vocation. It has to be made, and it has to be made before a certain date-line. There comes a time when the plunge must be taken. And under these limitations of time and evidence, the only thing to do is to obtain what light one can, and then *decide*.

In the field of practical politics, it is necessary to make decisions on the ground of evidence that no

scientific expert would consider sufficient. The statesman cannot leave matters undecided, or postpone his
decision indefinitely and bequeath the problem to
later investigators. There is a story about the late
President Roosevelt that illustrates the point. It is
said that when he had a certain measure before him,
he called in an economic expert and presented the
problem. This expert, obeying his scientific scruples,
presented the evidence pro and con—"on the one
hand," and "on the other hand." When this had gone
on for some time, President Roosevelt, according to
the story, lost patience, and said, "Now look here—if
you were like me, just a ham politician, and had
either to sign or to veto this bill before 12 o'clock to-
morrow, what would you do?" Exit expert.

As citizens in a democracy, we are all in the position of the official of government, though our responsibility is less crushing. Even if we do nothing but
vote, we have to make up our minds before election
day on questions about which we are largely ignorant, and to which no one on earth has an exact and
certain answer. Even voting may not be an act of
choice, as is implied when we make light of that ac-
clamation of which totalitarian countries boast. Political decision is not "tossing up for it," or following another's example, or doing what one is told or
paid for; it is a conclusion drawn from some exami-
nation of the merits of the question. It is a deciding
for oneself—unless one is to let someone else decide;

and there are always those who are ready to relieve one of the burden.

The distinguished philosopher, Bertrand Russell, has written of one of his books: "The net result is to substitute articulate hesitation for inarticulate certainty. Whether this result has any value is a question which I shall not consider." [3] The author might well have doubts of the value of his book if its only result was to create hesitation. It is a good thing to hesitate before adopting ideas, but there is little good (except in a now obsolete form of the waltz) in continuing to hesitate. It is a good thing to "look before you leap"; not, however, to keep on looking, but to *look and then leap*. There is a better phrase than Russell's "articulate hesitation": it is "judiciously credulous," supplied by Joseph Glanvill.[4] To Voltaire is attributed the maxim, "Read not to believe but to consider"—to which might be added "Consider not to doubt but to decide."

I am suggesting three things. First, that our minds are meant to guide our action. Second, that our minds cannot guide our action unless we make them up. And third, I am suggesting that we are obliged to make up our minds on many fundamental matters, including politics, as best we can, without conclusive evidence of a sort which the question theoretically requires.

What should the teacher try to do about it? I suggest that there is what might be called an "art of decision"—an act of commitment following an interval of non-commitment. The teacher should help his student to learn this art. First, he should practice it himself. The teacher who makes no decisions is evading the hardest part of the task. It is comparatively easy to raise doubts, to point out the ignorance and conflicting evidence that beset the mind on every side. It is well to do this—an honest and trained mind will do it. I would not abolish or disparage the critical part of teaching. But doubt should be regarded as the prelude to belief; or, as we say, criticism should be constructive, and not merely destructive. If beliefs are demolished, they should be built again, or others built in their place. If this is not done, the vacuum will be filled by authority, hearsay, or superstition.

And then, having exhibited the art of decision, the teacher should help his students to reach their own decisions, to make up their own minds. This is something very different from proselytism. It is respectful of other minds; it is both scrupulous and modest. But at the same time, it is responsible. It is an attempt to assist those whose minds have been awakened to doubt, but are suffering from indecision through being ignorant of the way in which to make decisions.

Let me add that decision does not always imply irrevocable decision. Sometimes it does, as when its occasion will never arise again. More often the question is a continuing question. The man who makes up his own mind may change it. Belief closes the mind but does not lock or seal it; it is a room with a door, and not a drafty corridor.

A second article of his self-imposed code that seriously limits the teacher's training of citizens is his reluctance to be explicit on the question of value. It is a truism that modern technology is as useful for bad as for good purposes. A report entitled *How Writers Perpetuate Stereotypes,* prepared in 1945 for a Writers' War Board,[5] examined the effect of short stories, the stage, motion pictures, radio programs, newsreels and advertising copy, on race prejudice. The conclusion reached was that the most "liberal" of these media was the stage, and that "the worst offender was the short story." But the racist could use the same data and invert the order of merit. Who is to teach the student or the public to prefer liberalism to racism?

A distinguished sociologist, in reviewing a work dealing with personnel problems in the American army, made the following comment:

These volumes depict science being used with great skill to sort out and to control men for purposes not of their own willing. It is a significant measure of the impotence of liberal democracy that it must increasingly use its social sciences not directly on democracy's own problems, but tangentially and indirectly; it must pick up the crumbs from private business research on such problems as how to gauge audience reaction so as to put together profitable synthetic radio programs to turn frightened draftees into tough soldiers who will fight a war whose purposes they do not understand.

What kind of society would that society be which developed its skills not on war but on the problems of peace; not by discovering how to lessen men's fear in battle but how to lessen the massive insecurities of civilian life; not by developing the synthetic morale of an army but the living tissue of democratic social solidarity; not in the hopeless search for palliatives for the caste gulf between officers and men, but in discovering the optimum conditions of responsible democratic relations among men of different capacities and roles.[6]

It is evident that this writer is on the side of liberalism, peace and "responsible democratic relations," but even he does not here suggest that these things be taught. He suggests no way in which American society can be induced to prefer the better to the worse use of social techniques.

The difficulty lies in the fact that social "science" no longer embraces knowledge of the good. Values are left to personal "attitudes," and to tamper with these is to expose the teacher to the charge of that "indoctrination" so notoriously exemplified by totalitarianism. It is a point of honor with the scholar that while the mind should be taught to examine evidence and weigh opposing arguments, and even to draw conclusions, this must be done without at any point insinuating a creed.

To press this scruple beyond a certain point is to lose sight of several incontestable facts. The minds of men are exposed not merely to evidence but to the creeds of other men, and it is utterly impossible to escape their imprint. There is, furthermore, an early period in the life of each individual—a period of ten or more years—when he is as yet incapable of thinking for himself, but when his life must nevertheless be guided by a creed. A man can reach thoughtful conclusions only when his mind is already furnished with ideas thoughtlessly acquired. As a rule thinking is re-thinking. Hence, the most that is possible is to enable the individual to re-examine, criticize, and revise or keep, convictions antecedently implanted.

Finally, and no less important, there is the fact that no teacher can withhold the influence of his own moral convictions. Teachers are not, and should not be, intellectual eunuchs. The most scrupulous re-specter of the freedom of other minds will, the more scrupulous he is, convert his students or his public to his own scrupulousness. The rightful freedom of minds, the maxims of consistency and experimental proof, of intellectual honesty, of tolerance and persuasion, are themselves a creed. Together with their personal and social implications they constitute a body of indoctrination to which no objection can consistently be raised, for he who objects is in that very act indoctrinating.

Here, I believe, is the reconciliation of the teacher's scruples with his obligation to implant a love of freedom in his students. Let him look for the ground on which he repudiates indoctrination. If he is *against* it, it is because, fundamentally, he is *for* something. What is this positive end which is implicit in his protest?

It will not do to say that he prefers some other rigid and narrow creed. A Communist critique of Nazi indoctrination, or a Nazi critique of Communist indoctrination, or a parental, scholastic, or dogmatic religious critique of both, would not go to the root of the matter. What the scrupulous teacher objects to is not the specific content of the creed which is rigidly and narrowly inculcated, but its rigidity and narrowness, whatever the specific content. To find the positive side of his scruples we must look for the opposites of *these* ideas, not Communism *vs* Nazism, or Nazism *vs* Communism, or religious dogma *vs* atheism, or filial piety *vs* domestic anarchy, but flexibility *vs* rigidity, breadth *vs* narrowness, freedom *vs* arbitrary compulsion.

Freedom of the mind, as preparation for the rôle of citizenship in a democracy, defines an educational purpose that can be methodically and consistently pursued, and that must be methodically and consistently pursued if it is to be achieved. The great weakness of the liberal's educational program lies in its failure to make plain the positive creed which underlies its negations. This is a special case of the weakness of liberalism in general. It protests against every species of authority, rigidity, and narrowness—

in the name of *what*? It hesitates to say, lest it seem to fall itself into illiberality. But the result of this excess of scrupulousness is that it has nothing to offer in place of the authorities and dogmas which it has weakened; and so it paves the way for other authorities and dogmas which it is bound to find equally objectionable. And because it fails to proclaim a positive end of its own, it lacks that purposefulness which springs from conviction and enthusiasm.

Freedom is a lesson that can be taught in every class-room—not only in courses *on* freedom, but in courses taught by the method of freedom, and by a teacher who exemplifies freedom. It is true that the greater part of education must invoke authority, the authority, namely, of knowledge. Only a portion of mankind has the capacity or leisure to understand the evidence for the truth of nuclear physics, or the theory of relativity, or the principles of heredity, or the geological age of the earth, or the chemical composition of celestial bodies, or the historical causes of the French Revolution. If the educated man's beliefs were limited to those which he can prove for himself, the effect of education would be to impoverish the mind; the educated man would be more ignorant than the man on the street who borrows his beliefs freely from others.

But at the same time that education thus invokes authority, it can define authority itself in terms of freedom. The ultimate personal authority in science—

the physicist, the biologist, the geologist, the chemist, the historian—does not himself accept authority, but reaches his conclusions freely in the light of evidence. So the layman who accepts such authority profits by another's freedom, and owes to freedom his indirect allegiance. He may traverse the discovery of truth in some small portion of his study, and be a lover of truth in all.

To become a teacher of freedom, the true scholar in any field of inquiry need do no more than avow and make plain the maxims which he is pledged to obey: the maxims of sincerity, veracity, objectivity, universality, open-mindedness and tolerance. There is no reason why he should be reticent in disclosing this code, since it makes no private claims in his own behalf, but enrolls him in the company of those who create an impersonal body of certified knowledge which is to become the possession of mankind at large.

Teachers and students engaged together in the exercise and cultivation of the art of thinking and deciding for oneself constitute that peculiar community of freedom which describes, or should describe, the American college and university. Spending a few years in this community, breathing its atmosphere, sharing its life, and becoming consciously aware of its meaning, should make its graduates the champions and models of enlightened and independent citizenship in their later lives. If they compose only a small portion of society, they should leaven the whole and thus repay the peculiar privilege which they have enjoyed.

The question of "academic freedom" has become a lively issue, owing to the spread from state to state of the example set by congressional committees which were created, originally, to protect the minds of Americans against the contamination of subversive ideas. This question should be divorced from the badness or wrongness of particular politico-economic doctrines such as Communism, and from the illegalities of treason, sabotage, or perjury. It is assumed that freedom of thought and expression should stop at the point where it immediately and unmistakably verges on revolutionary violence. For present purposes, the question is further limited to the peculiar case of the academic community, where scholars who are supposed to teach meet students who are supposed to learn.

There are those who believe that this academic situation calls for a peculiar watchfulness, lest freedom be abused, and there are those who believe that it calls for a peculiar tolerance and encouragement, lest freedom be strangled in its cradle or die of starvation. In some institutions, and from time to time in all institutions, the question becomes acute when inquisitive students would like to invite to the sacred precincts some "outside speaker" with doubtful credentials.

On the one hand, there are those who believe that young people in their late teens and early twenties should be protected against dangerous thoughts. The college or university, according to this view, should be a nursery, where tender plants are protected against the rough winds of conflicting ideas. In a desperate attempt to find a compromise, some academic authorities have adopted a rule that no public speaker, or at any rate outsider, shall be allowed to deal with what are called "controversial" topics. It is assumed that later on, when the young have matured and toughened, it will then be safe to expose them. There are some, of course, who believe that that time never comes, and who would enlarge the nursery to accommodate Americans of all ages.

According to the opposite view, the view to which we are here committed, the place in all the world in which it is most proper to deal with controversial subjects is the college or university; and of all periods in the individual's life, youth is the period when this encounter with controversial subjects is most natural and profitable.

For the sake of emphasis let me state this position somewhat extravagantly. First, all thinking is dangerous, if by "dangerous" is meant the possibility of arriving at opinions different from those which prevail in the community. Second, all important questions are controversial, if by "controversial" is meant that there are at least two sides that can conceivably be taken. If two sides are not already taken, the attempt to suppress a question on the ground that it is controversial will make it controversial.

Third, assuming that thinking somewhere at some time is desirable, there is more likelihood that the individual will think in his youth than later in life. If he does not begin to think then, he may never think. After graduation he finds himself more and more committed. His mind becomes more and more dominated by the opinions of his professional or business associates, or by his religion, economic class, or political party, or by the agencies of mass communication. He becomes less and less apt to think and rethink his beliefs. Youth is the period of untrammelled curiosity, when the mind is most receptive to ideas. The college or university is designed to stimulate and develop this aptitude—to provide the tools and materials of thought at the time when the individual is most disposed to use them.

I am not unaware of the difficulty which the creed of freedom creates for educational authorities who have to worry about financial support—whether from a legislature or from alumni. There is, however, only one solution of this difficulty—the only ultimate solution, and the only American solution; namely, to educate those who provide the support, so that they can better understand what it is that they support. At present, the privately-endowed institutions enjoy, in this respect, an advantage over the state-supported institutions. Whereas the latter are governed by regents, legislatures and the electorate-at-large, privately-endowed institutions are governed by trustees and alumni, who can be assumed to feel a closer sympathy with the purposes and principles of higher education.

But this is an ephemeral and at best a relative advantage. The state electorate is composed more and more of alumni of state colleges and universities; the alumni of privately-endowed colleges and universities are dispersed and absorbed in the electorate, and tend to be of the same mind. In self-defense, as well as to fulfill their obligation of public service, all institutions of higher education must therefore educate not only their own students, but the people at large, to value such institutions for that unique service which they alone are qualified to render.

They must not be expected to be retreats for the tender-minded, clubs for the privileged, factories for the manufacture of standardized products, or even training centers for specialists, but communities of freedom where the art of freedom is taught, practiced, learned, and so deeply implanted as to last for life.

Insofar as this idea is realized, the college and university will no longer be cloistered from the surrounding world. The seat of learning designed to prepare men for democracy will have become a microcosm of democracy. There will be no abrupt change when the student becomes a citizen. He will carry with him the poise and self-mastery of one who, having drawn to himself all possible rays of light, will be competent to make enlightened decisions.

CHAPTER VII

THE BAD REPUTATION OF MORALITY

Disraeli is quoted as having said that "Gladstone is a good man in the worst sense of the word." To be called "good," or "virtuous," or "dutiful" is a doubtful compliment. This bad reputation of morality is largely responsible for the omission of moral education from the modern educational program, or the reluctance, at any rate, to call it "moral." On the face of it, this is absurd. The important thing about a man is his conduct, or his set of dispositions. Even what he thinks bears fruit in what he does; thinking itself is a kind of doing or being disposed to do.

We pay lip-service to the importance of morality, and are convinced of its importance. We know that society is threatened at home by the conflict between employment and labor, and that the only possible solution of the problem is a moral solution. We know that dishonesty and corruption gnaw at the vitals of our system of life and have made us an object of scorn to that Communism to which we feel ourselves so superior. We know that political democracy is debased by the development of the mass-mind, and that the only salvation of democracy is to instill in the people a love of truth and a capacity to find it amidst a welter of propaganda and misinformation. We know that our precious civil liberties are perpetually jeopardized and often destroyed because our people lack the virtue of tolerance. We realize that the developments of natural science, culminating in nuclear physics, threaten to destroy mankind; and that they can be converted to good rather than bad uses, only if they are subjected to a moral control. We live under the horrid threat of a war in which all mankind may go down together, and we know that the only escape lies in implanting good will and the spirit of justice in the hearts of men. We know all these things, and we repeatedly proclaim them.

What do we do about it? What do educators do to prepare the minds of youth to meet these requirements? Schools, colleges, and universities, designed expressly for educational purposes, attempt little, leaving the major task to the home, the church, the Boy or Girl Scouts, or other more impromptu organizations. But even these agencies hesitate to assume full responsibility. The church passes it on to the home, and the home passes it back to the church. The Protestant churches, especially those of liberal persuasion, tend to an increasing extent to leave these problems to their members to work out for themselves, lest their personal independence be violated. Even the Catholic Church, pledged to inculcate a moral code, and less fearful of dogma and authority, places its chief emphasis on religious observance and personal conduct rather than on civic virtue. Great as is the rôle of the churches in the field of moral education, there are many, even among church members, who do not go to church. And even among those who attend, the number of hours spent in church is trifling in comparison with the hours spent in school, college, and university.

Where in the curriculum or other organized activities of secondary and higher education does the training of the moral will and implanting of moral sentiments find a place? Perhaps in occasional so-called "inspirational" addresses delivered in the chapel or at assemblies and convocations. But the very fact that moral education is extra-curricular creates a sense of its unimportance.*

It will be noted that the neglect of moral education is often due not to its difficulty, but to the highest motives. Teachers hesitate to tamper with the wills of their students because the will is a central and vital organ. They hesitate to touch it for fear that they will injure it—which is precisely as though the physician or surgeon should limit himself to treating

*It is to be noted that Catholic colleges for the most part require a course on "natural ethics;" and that in some cases, under the topic of "justice," considerable attention is given to civic morals.

the common cold or to setting minor fractures, and refuse to treat the brain or the heart. Or teachers hesitate to engage in moral education out of respect for the rights of the individual. But if this respect for individual rights is the unspoken premise of educational practice, why should it not be spoken, and why should students not be expressly and methodically taught to feel it?

Morality is also the premise, usually unspoken, of social organization. A recent Report of the Advisory Council on Education in Scotland found that "Children must learn that the things that bring all men together are greater than the things that keep them apart," and that the teachers must have "a firm grasp of moral principles, even accepting the risk that these may be called prejudices." [1] The remark that the moral teacher must take the risk of being considered "prejudiced" is revealing. Morality, in the shape of will and character, *is* a prejudice. But the use of this word suggests that it is a petty eccentricity, an arbitrary peculiarity, like preferring blonds to brunettes or French dressing to mayonnaise; whereas if morality means that "the things that bring men together are greater than the things that keep them apart," as indeed it does, then it underlies all human institutions, including education itself.

The moralizer is viewed with alarm by his victims; and he himself shrinks from assuming the rôle unless it can be called by some other name. Some of the reasons for this declining repute of morality are trivial and have to do with merely verbal associations, or with transitory manners and customs; these reasons need not concern us. There are other reasons, however, which spring from the nature of morality itself, and reveal its true meaning. There are reasons why morality, being what it is, should have become identified in the popular mind with certain distortions of itself—known, and rightly known, by bad names: *asceticism, authoritarianism, preceptualism* and *utopianism.*

Asceticism arises from the fact that morality goes against the grain. Its forward drive springs from the interests which it harmonizes, its purpose being to save these interests from weakness and mutual destruction: morality is for the sake of the harmonized. But in order that interests shall be harmonized, they must be modified and realigned. There would be no need of harmonizing them if they were harmonious as they stood. Furthermore, the elements to be reorganized are not passive materials to be manipulated at will by an external agency; each is an *interest,* which moves to action or to inertia on its own account. Hence, it resists being deflected from its own particular end, and the harmonizing force has to overcome this resistance, which is sometimes known as "original sin."

This overcoming of resistance, because it is tense and dramatic, draws attention to itself, and is taken to be the substance rather than the accident. Because the resistance of the original interests must be overcome, morality comes to be identified with their defeat. Because the harmony of the whole is obliged to oppose itself to particular inclinations, morality comes to be identified with *dis*inclination. Hence arises the perverted ethics of asceticism, self-denial, mortification of the flesh, and duty for duty's sake.

This view of morality as the mere subjugation of nature is explicable, but it is nevertheless monstrous. For the purpose of morality is to save, not to destroy. If interests are confined, it is not to starve them, but to make room for them, in order that they may flourish more abundantly. Natural impulses are to be tamed and curbed, but without breaking their spirit. Morality is a bridle, and not a procrustean bed. It is designed to free, and not to torture, the flesh which it contains and limits. The last word of morality is not "no" but "yes."

The ill repute of morality is due, in the first place, then, to its being conceived as a negation of life. Although it is designed to be the best friend of every interest, desire, and aspiration, it comes to be viewed as their common enemy. The natural appetites, ambition, pleasure, passion, aesthetic and intellectual enjoyments, align themselves against it.

A second aspect of morality is its sanction by authority. The harmony of interests, imposed on interests for their own benefit, is assigned to some commanding will, such as God, the civil ruler, the priest, or the parent—a being who is supposed to know best, and to have a power of enforcement. Virtue and right conduct then assume the form of obedience.

Nature has provided for a period of dependence and tutelage at the beginning of every individual's life. Every man begins as a child, and as a child learns morality at his mother's, or across his father's, knee; and it is tinged with indulgence or severity by these parental channels. Similarly, the social group learns morality at the dawn of its history through the spokesman for its tutelary deity. The Ten Commandments were given to Moses and his people by the Lord their God, amidst "the thunderings, the lightnings, and the noise of the trumpet, and the mountain smoking." [2]

Thus, what men ought to do is conceived as what they are bribed to do, or what they are afraid not to do. For the essence of morality—justice and co-öperation—is substituted its accident of reward or penalty. And the authority itself is conceived as an arbitrary will to be appeased. So to conceive authority is to forget that power corrupts, and would corrupt even God, were He not governed by moral principles other than that of the "passive obedience" which is sometimes supposed to be demanded of His human subjects. If God Himself is just and benevolent in the absence of commands from a superior being, there is no reason why man, in his adult years and in his human and finite degree, should not be the same.

Nothing, surely, could be more fantastic than to define morality in terms of immaturity, incapacity, and dependence—in terms of that stage of social or individual development when men have to be made to do what they ought to do. Morality is then something to be outgrown and discarded, together with other childish things, by grown men. As a counsel of sheer submission, it allies itself with every species of tyranny and draws upon itself the united condemnation of the champions of freedom and self-reliance.

A third aspect of morality is its formulation of precepts. Morality, like all systems, has its rules; and if its harmonizing purpose is to be realized, these rules must be generally respected and obeyed. These rules commonly originate as the commands of an authority, and when the authority is eliminated they assume the form of taboos, maxims, aphorisms, and axioms, which retain an authoritarian flavor. This is also inescapable, as the sequel to a fading authority. Thus, the Ten Commandments were inscribed on tablets of stone, and afterwards in a sacred book. When God and Moses were forgotten, the rules themselves were still expressed in the imperative voice—"thou shalt," "thou shalt not"—which echoed the thunder and the trumpet, and still smelled of smoke. Duty, "the stern daughter of the voice of God," continues to speak sternly when God withdraws to the background. The commands of parents never wholly lose their parental associations even when children have left the home.

Morality thus comes to be identified with ready-made precepts, such as the Golden Rule, or the standardized virtues—justice, courage, wisdom, temperance, faith, hope, love, prudence, veracity, honesty or unselfishness—which stand by themselves as absolutes. Their echo of authority seems to come from their own reflecting surfaces. They become divorced from their meaning as principles by which the good life is realized, both in persons and in societies.

The identification of morality with a set of stereotyped precepts is one of the main causes of its disrepute. So conceived, it becomes legalistic and casuistical, and strict observance of the rule is substituted for humane feeling. The precept becomes rigid and sacrosanct, enshrining the errors and limitations of the time in which it became current, and impervious to personal judgment and advancing enlightenment. Here is what George Eliot had to say on the subject:

All people of broad, strong sense have an instinctive repugnance to the men of maxims; because such people early discover that the mysterious complexity of our life is not to be embraced by maxims, and that to lace ourselves up in formulas of that sort is to repress all the divine prompt-ings and inspirations that spring from growing insight and sympathy. And the man of maxims is the popular representative of the minds that are guided in their moral judgment solely by general rules, thinking that these will lead them to justice by a ready-made patent method, without the trouble of exerting patience, discrimination, impartiality—without any care to assure themselves whether they have the insight that comes from a hardly-earned estimate of temptation, or from a life vivid and intense enough to have created a wide fellow-feeling with all that is human.[3]

The preceptive moralist teaches morality by uttering pious platitudes and Sunday School edification, which are dismissed with contempt by the men who grapple with the concrete difficulties of life. He exhorts, scolds, utters anathemas, pronounces bans and threats—from finger-shaking to inquisition. He is like the umpire who calls fouls and applies penalties, without participating in the game; or like the teacher who merely polices the classroom where others work. He is resented as both external and meddlesome.

It is necessary to learn the moral rules and win men to their acceptance, but through overinsistence on their abstract form morality makes enemies of those who ought to be its friends; those, namely, who are most eager to do the right in some concrete personal, family, social, or international situation. He who is exhorted to be just, honorable, kind, generous and unselfish, or to love his neighbor as himself, will want to know just how such precepts apply, and to discover this he must cast off the spell of the bare rule, and undertake the task of living with himself and with his neighbors.

A fourth reason for the ill repute of morality is its so-called "utopianism." The divorce between imaginary perfection and the actual state of affairs is inevitable; it is a part, though not the whole, of the moral process. The moral organization of life is directed to a goal, and it is necessary to form an idea of the goal. To clarify the idea and fix it in men's minds, it is necessary that it should be imagined. To vivify its ideal meaning, the moralist will play the rôle of poet and dream of a harmonious society—a State of Nature, a terrestrial or celestial Paradise, a realm of angels, saints, and redeemed persons—whose members are just, benevolent, and coöperative, and in which the happiness of each is embraced within the happiness of all.

But utopianism tempts men to substitute the dreaming of dreams for the task of reshaping existence and controlling the course of events. When morality is so conceived, it loses the confidence of men of action, who look upon it as an evasion. The work of the world is then carried on under some other banner, such as "practicality" or "realism." It is a sound instinct, morally sound, which prompts men to feel that there is more of morality in a single step forward against the resistance of the present state of affairs than in a lifetime spent enjoying the image of perfection. For morality consists not in the contemplation of the best, but in the achievement of the best possible; it defines a direction and goal of effort. It is not a leap, but a continuous movement. Morality must keep its eye on the distant goal, but it is also morality to which we must look for traversing the intermediate distance, however long it may be, and however beset with obstacles.

When morality is thus conceived as a goal, it encounters a familiar objection concerning means and ends. Our opponents in the cold war are charged with holding the false doctrine that "the end justifies the means." On the face of it, this is a strange objection: for what could justify a means if not its end. The means is the means *to* something, and if it enables him who chooses it to reach that something, or to move in its direction, it is well chosen.

The objection may then be restated so as to deny that morality is a means at all, and to affirm that its value lies in what it is in itself, and not in its consequences. But this also is a strange doctrine. For are not justice, benevolence, veracity, temperance and all the other familiar forms of morality roads to happiness and social well-being, and are they not prized on that account? Is it not that to which we appeal when we urge their adoption?

There remains another and more valid view of the objection. According to this view, if the means is to be finally justified, the end by which it is justified must be the highest end. A successful means to an end might well be condemned despite its success, if the end itself were evil, or, if it conflicted with a higher end. Thus mendacity and ruthlessness may be the way to power and conquest, but they violate truth and humane feeling, which are the way to the end of universal happiness.

Even devotion to a remote, ideal end may violate its own ideal through neglect of immediate consequences, and through hardening the hearts of its devotees. There is an evil in fanaticism, no matter what its object may be.* A convert from Communism, Louis Fischer, has said: "In one's absorption with an ideal, it is possible to imagine that one generation may be sacrificed for its descendants. But sacrificing people may become a habit into the third and fourth generation." [4]

A good thing perpetually postponed is only a negation. Universal happiness, or the welfare of man-

---

*The relation between the moral end and the moral means should not, strictly speaking, be conceived as an external relation. The means is often a part of the end, and not an antecedent. It may, therefore, be argued that no means is morally justified which violates the end. This view, however, would not account for the cases in which war is necessarily employed as a means to peace, or capital punishment as a means to the preservation of life, or imprisonment as a means to freedom. There is no escape from this dilemma except by saying that *so far as possible* the means selected shall be such as to agree with the end. It is one of the chronic difficulties of the moral life that the realization of the end requires present action which would be excluded were the end realized.

kind, includes the present as well as the future. Thomas Jefferson said, "The Earth belongs always to the living generation." [5] It is not necessary to deny the claims of the generations to come, but the earth and its fruits, and the achievements of man, belong *at least* to the living.

If morality is to be given its rightful place in human life, it must be freed from those distortions and caricatures, those substitutions of a part for the whole, in which the literature and discourse of morality abound, and by which it has created and armed its enemies. It must cease to seem merely negative, authoritarian, platitudinous, utopian, irrelevant to the immediate and concrete business of life, and be recognized instead as the vital necessity which it really is. As an individual or a society matures, morality becomes less and less a matter of resisting the temptations of the flesh, or obeying the wise and powerful, or conforming to rules and regulations, or lying down in the green pastures beside the still waters of the imagination, or postponing the good to the distant future. It is seen to be man's perpetual effort, beginning here and now, to organize his life and substitute coöperation for conflict.

CHAPTER VIII

CIVIC MORALS IN A DEMOCRACY

In 1897 William James delivered an oration at the unveiling of a monument to Robert Gould Shaw, who had been killed at the head of a colored regiment in the Civil War. There are, said the orator, two kinds of courage, for both of which Colonel Shaw was to be honored: the fighting courage of a soldier, and the moral courage of the good citizen. The former is more conspicuous, but the latter is more necessary:

The deadliest enemies of nations are not their foreign foes; they always dwell within their borders. And from these internal enemies civilization is always in need of being saved. The nation blest above all nations is she in whom the civic genius of the people does the saving day by day, by acts without external picturesqueness; by speaking, writing, voting reasonably; by smiting corruption swiftly; by good temper between parties; by the people knowing true men when they see them, and preferring them as leaders to rabid partisans or empty quacks.[1]

Some doubt exists in the minds of Americans today whether this nation is thus "blest." The Senate Committee on Banking and Currency, under the chairmanship of Senator J. W. Fulbright of Arkansas, has recently submitted a *Study of the Reconstruction Finance Corporation,* in which it appears that this body has been guilty of "favoritism and influence" in making federal loans to private business. More recently, a Special Committee to Investigate Organized Crime in Interstate Commerce, under the chairmanship of Senator Estes Kefauver of Tennessee, has revealed, in the glare of television, the fact that "organized criminal gangs operating in interstate commerce are firmly entrenched in our large cities in the operation of many different gambling enterprises such as bookmaking, policy, slot machines, as well as in other rackets such as the sale and distribution of narcotics and commercialized prostitution." [2]

These two reports deal with different forms of evildoing, but they both relate to political standards. The Fulbright Report deals with "improper" conduct on the part of federal officials and certain improper influences which have been brought to bear upon them. We are told of the "pull" and the "influence pedlar," of nepotism and favors given for favors received. The question of legality is not raised, except to say that something *more* than mere legality should be expected of persons in positions of trust. The Kefauver Report, on the other hand, deals with law-breakers, but at the same time emphasizes the connivance of the law enforcement agencies, known as the "fix."

Both reports, therefore, drive home the necessity of raising the level of civic morality.

These two reports came at a time when the American public had already been shocked by other events and "revelations." People had not forgotten the days of bootlegging, or even of Teapot Dome. They had heard of the "five-percenters" and lobbyists, who sold to their clients the personal "contacts" they had acquired as office-holders in Washington. The election of 1950 had been exceptionally bitter, even as judged by American standards, and the next election threatened to be worse. The McCarthy episode, coming after the performances of the Dies Committee and its successors, had shaken popular faith in the protection of ancient rights, and convinced many people that some members of Congress used their immunities to destroy their personal or political enemies. The perpetual wrangling between the Executive and the Congress had injured the general reputation of government for disinterested public service.

In view of these and similar experiences, it would not be strange if Americans, as of 1951, had come to feel a sense of shame and indignation. There is, of course, that last consolation, namely, the recollection that things have been as bad or worse before. The recent abuse of political opponents, we are told, is mild as compared with the actions of the press in Lincoln's time:

Scurrilous and defamatory stories about Roosevelt were circulated largely by word of mouth: but Lincoln was accused openly of drawing his salary in gold while his soldiers were paid in greenbacks, of being drunk when he wrote a state paper, of granting pardons to military rebels in order to procure votes for his second election, of being guilty of "wholesale murder," of being "a perjured traitor." [3]

We are also accustomed to refer to the periodicity of corruption and reform in America—with special reference to the ups and downs of Tammany Hall. But while it would be pleasant to believe that "whatever goes down always comes up," the law of gravitation would suggest the opposite—that "whatever goes up always comes down"—and that sometime it *may* come down for the last time.

The records of the past do, it is true, argue against the despairing view that the country is morally on the downgrade. But lest we become too complacent, it is well to bear in mind that there are at least two new factors which add to the gravity of the present situation. The first of these is the development of the arts of mass communication. This factor may be argued both ways. Mass communication spreads influences far and wide, and tends to a solidarity of opinion and feeling. Evil-doing in public places is not allowed to hide itself, and if it is condemned the force of popular condemnation is magnified. The assumption that a public conscience will be aroused when the facts are made known underlies the argument for televising the proceedings of the Kefauver Committee. If, however, the attitude is one of cynical acceptance, or of morbid curiosity, or if the exposure of evil becomes a spectacle enjoyed by the audience and used by the principals of the cast to advance their political interests or gratify their exhibitionism, then mass communication degrades, and does not raise, the moral standards of the public.

The second factor which contributes to the gravity of our present domestic malady is our new international responsibility. Our leadership requires moral, as well as military and economic, leadership. Our chief competitor, the Communist bloc led by Soviet Russia, claims with some justice to have raised the standards of public service. There is evidence that the Communist régime in China has eliminated the "squeeze" (which in America is called "graft") despite the fact that this has, from time immemorial, been an established Oriental practice. The régime of Chiang Kai-shek was rejected as corrupt, and Chinese Communists are now disposed to point the same accusing finger at America. Communism is itself highly vulnerable on moral grounds, having both professed and practiced the propagation of lies and the suborning of trusted officials as techniques of revolution. But how can we profit by this moral advantage at a time when our own moral guilt is so evident?

Corruption is a cause not only of evil reputation, but also of weakness. We cannot be strong either at home or in the world at large by the method of "favoritism and influence," or by violating our own creed of justice, tolerance, and equal opportunity, or still less by a partnership between crime and law enforcement.

There are many causes of the present low state of public morals in America, some of which spring from what is most characteristic of the American mentality, tradition, and system of life. The art of large-scale operation, learned in business, is readily transferred to crime. Control of vast enterprises by a few individuals, sometimes "insiders" subject to no accounting, sometimes men of wealth conspicuous for their extravagant expenditures, is known in both areas. Crime, like all business in America, tends to become big business. The "mobster," the "gangster," and the "racketeer" are the criminal counterparts of the ruthless monopolist. The Kefauver Report says of organized crime that "the amounts of money involved are so tremendous that the expenditure of large sums of money for corruption of enforcement officials, and officials at even higher levels, can and is absorbed as an expense of doing business." [4] Is there perhaps some hint here of the expenditures for lobbying or "educating" the public which are absorbed as an expense of doing business by public utility and other corporations?

In any case it cannot be denied that graft and organized crime reflect the tone of certain questionable business practices that are condoned in the community at large. It is comparatively easy to place the responsibility on the (usually underpaid) official; but the general public is responsible for his elevation to office and for the disesteem in which he is held. No one is bribed without a briber, but the giver of bribes is considered "respectable." Influence would not command a price if there were no one willing to pay for it. The representative in Congress who engages in logrolling or other practices contrary to the public interest is obeying what he takes to be the will of his constituents. Few constituents of a congressman or senator would hesitate to ask favors of him, or to vote for him in return for favors given and promised.

In the end, the fault lies with the public conscience of America, and there is no American who can escape responsibility. Our spirit of good-fellowship, admirable as it is, tends to soften our moral judgment. The friendliness which exchanges favors asks few questions. Even after we have been swept by patriotic passion and have girded our loins for a great collective effort, as in time of war, we soon grow weary of righteousness. We feel that we have earned an era of Harding after the unnatural strain of an era of Wilson.

We are a greedy and spoiled people, which is no more than the natural effect of our wealth. We are accustomed to having what we want, such as beef and automobiles. Our private appetites resist any control in the interest of public policy. Most of organized crime springs from the violation of laws which deny to large groups of people things which they are accustomed to enjoy and to which they have come to believe they have a right. Prohibition and bootlegging afford the classic example in America. The resistance to peacetime rationing and price-control is an ominously significant sign at the present time. It has been rightly attributed by a "spokesman" in Washington to "a breakdown in public morality."

The present corruption of "amateur" athletes expresses another profoundly American characteristic —the worship of "success," no matter how it is achieved, so long as it is competitive and spectacular. Similarly, the fabulously successful criminal, though he is condemned, becomes something of a popular hero. Trial by jury tends to become a battle of wits and rhetoric between opposing lawyers, and in the practice of criminal law there is often glory for the winner, regardless of the guilt or innocence of the defendant. It is this which creates doubts as to the moral effect of the television hearings of the Kefauver Committee. Is not some of the popular applause received by the Committee due to its having "put on a good show"—better than any fictitious melodrama? Insofar as crime "adds to the excitement," and is just another form of mass entertain-

ment, it arouses no moral indignation. Its evil consequences—its threat to the integrity of American life—
are overlooked and forgotten.

Why do people read crime news with such avidity?
Why does "sensational" news command so high a
price? Not because people want to know the disease
in order to cure it. In the mass of readers it stirs no
impulse of reform; on the contrary, they enjoy it.
They enjoy it in part because, like pornography, it
provides a secret gratification of their own appetites.
In part they enjoy it because of an unattractive trait
which Americans share with the rest of mankind. The
"exposure" of crime, especially on the part of known
persons, satisfies a morbid curiosity. Like scandal, it
causes a certain "ghoulish glee." Perhaps the guilt of
others flatters one's own sense of merit.

Lapses in the public conscience are due, in no small
degree, to the general failure to recognize morality
for what it really is. It tends to be considered as
something apart from the issues of everyday life, and
therefore as something which, when it is introduced
into a situation, is irrelevant and intrusive. The essential meaning of morality tends to be lost, owing not
only to the distortions described in the previous chapter, but to the very richness of the moral vocabulary.
The different moral words have their stricter meanings, but tend in popular usage to be extended over
the whole of morality.

Thus, we say of any act which is morally disapproved that "it is a crime." But "crime," strictly speaking, is a comparatively serious breach of the civil law, as distinguished from a mere felony or misdemeanor. "Sin," on the other hand, owes its strict meaning to theology or metaphysics. It is a breach of the law of God, or an offense against man's deeper spiritual nature. Here, too, the stricter meaning is blurred in popular speech, and one may say "It is a sin" of any act which is disapproved. The terms "virtue" and "vice" have become identified in popular usage, especially in Protestant countries, with certain forms of misconduct which are taken to imply a too-ready yielding to natural appetites, or a "looseness" of life as opposed to discipline. Although these terms may be extended to apply to drunkenness, theatre-going, dancing, gambling, use of narcotics, or any other supposedly inordinate pursuit of pleasure, they tend to emphasize sex as being the most wanton of human passions. A woman's "virtue" signifies her chastity or marital fidelity, and the primary business of the "vice-squad" of the police force is to suppress prostitution. "Immorality," like "living in sin," commonly means nothing more or less than sexual intercourse unsanctioned by marriage.

This is more than a verbal matter. How can moral judgment be firm and enlightened, and how can morality be taught, corrected, and applied, if there is no agreement as to what "moral" means? How can men be morally condemned as guilty under one meaning, if they can excuse themselves or be acquitted by society under another? How can a dishonest politician or business man whose sex practices and church attendance are irreproachable be condemned as immoral if sexual and religious orthodoxy are taken to be the whole of morality? Where there are so many moralities there can be no morality, in the sense of a unified force or social conscience. When some people associate morality with control of appetite, others with obedience to formal laws imposed by a divine or civil ruler, others with a set of stereotyped precepts, and others with the pursuit of a distant ideal goal having no relation to present achievement, there is no common moral cause and no concerted moral action—but only confusion.

To clarify this situation, it is necessary to go to the heart of the matter of morality, and to understand that morality lies at the very core of life. It is a necessity imposed on man by the undeniable fact that his life, whether personal or social, is composed of a multitude of needs, wants, desires, and wills, which conflict with one another if they are allowed freely to run their several courses. Conflict breeds war—between the rival impulses of the same person, between the members of the same household, between one man's demands and his neighbors, between the interests of different classes within each society, and between the ambitions of the several nations and groups of nations that compose mankind. War leads to destruction—in the long run, to the destruction of all parties. Morality is the task of saving human life from this self-destruction. It is achieved, so far as it is achieved, by organization; that is, by creating an order of life which makes room for the several interests, and makes them partners rather than enemies.

In the otherwise admirable speech made in submitting his report, Senator Fulbright referred to "the totalitarian concept that the end justifies the means, a concept which is fundamentally and completely antagonistic to a true democratic society. Democracy is, I believe, more likely to be destroyed by the perversion of, or abandonment of, its true moral principles than by armed attack from Russia." [5] Does this not mean, does it not *say*, that democracy is saved by its "true moral principles"; is it not implied that this end is what justifies these "true moral principles," and that they are to be cherished on this account?

When morality is conceived as the saving of a democracy, and when democracy is conceived as an organization of society which gives the largest possible freedom to its personal members and to their personal interests, which encourages voluntary coöperation, and which extends these purposes to all societies and to their relations, then there is no longer any sharp dividing line between private and public morals, or between national and international morals. The same principles by which a man sets his own house in order apply to the ordering of the affairs of a nation and of mankind.

The major institutions of human society are all moral institutions, morality being rightly conceived. Polity, law, and economy are varieties of moral organization. It is the purpose of government to provide for the safety and well-being of all of those who live under it; it preserves order among them, and frames and enforces policies which will enable them to enjoy the fruits of coöperation. It seeks to promote peaceful and coöperative relations with other nations, for the good of all peoples concerned. Law defines and administers a system of justice, within which each man may know his rights and count upon their recognition by others. Economy organizes men's labor and resources so that needs can be met, and met abundantly, without resort to plunder. Each of these institutions makes its own peculiar contribution to society; all of them exist in order that men, impelled by their interests, may avoid the destructiveness of conflict, and achieve abundance through coördinated effort.

When these institutions are divorced from their common moral purpose, they cease to be public institutions, serving the good of society at large, and become mere careers ministering to private greed and ambition. Politics is politics! That is to say, politics means getting into office, staying in office, and "getting something out of it" for oneself and one's friends.

If one is condemned on moral grounds, one excuses oneself on the ground that politics hasn't anything to do with morality—which is true if morality means what it often is taken to mean. But if morality means setting the general good above selfish interests, then nothing could be more to the point. The politician who covets and uses an office of government for his private gain or power isn't doing the *political* job; he isn't a politician at all, any more than a so-called physician who practiced for the sake of his fees, regardless of the health of his patients, would be a real physician. Their own private profits are not what we have politicians and physicians *for*.

Law is the science and art of rules; not *any* rules, but rules of right and justice. In fact, these terms are used interchangeably with "law:" *droit* in French, *recht* in German, a "Department of Justice" in America. The legislators who make law, the courts which interpret and administer law, and the lawyers who "practice law" are all professionally dedicated to right and justice. But law, like any other social agency, has its mechanisms, and the law has its rewards for those for whom it provides a career and a livelihood. The procedures and instruments of law are so elaborate and have generated so many secondary motives that its fundamental moral purpose is easily forgotten.

For example: it is believed in America, and for good reasons, that justice requires that a man should be tried by a jury of his peers, and that each party (the prosecuting authority, the plaintiff, and above all the defendant) should be represented by lawyers whose duty is to plead his side of the case. As a consequence, *special* pleading and jury appeal are condoned by the professional legal code and highly rewarded by clients. This is not a question of honesty. The complaint is that in practice law tends to be deflected from its disinterested purpose of protecting rights and doing justice. Even judges, whose disinterestedness is highly respected, are usually men who have been practicing lawyers, and who will have acquired something of the practicing lawyer's habit of mind; and they are not immune to the influence of the opposing lawyers who present and argue the case before them. Even law schools whose faculties are supposed to be scholars in the law, and to understand its social function, are engaged in training practicing lawyers. They are the suppliers of the demand, and their success is likely to be judged by the practical success of their products.

While the purpose of the law (except for a limited area of arbitrary convention) is moral, it comprises only that small fraction of morality in which public regulation is necessary and expedient. Truthfulness, temperance, generosity, and love are not legalized. The greater part even of justice and right, as in the personal and domestic relations, fall within no jurisdiction. When morality is watered down to legality, and when the law itself is divested of its moral meaning, then legality provides a refuge for those who wish to escape morality altogether. Conscience is reduced to what one "can get away with"; as a result, there is no voice left which speaks for principles on which the good life, personal or social, depends.

Politicians, lawyers, and business men play the leading rôles in American life, and certainly the least of these is not the business man. The business man is the instrument of the economy, as the politician is the instrument of the state and the lawyer of the law; and, like these other functionaries, he is likely to forget his moral purpose. He does not usually deny this moral purpose. Call upon the business man to justify his profits or the harsh or shrewd practices of competition, and he will tell you that he satisfies the wants of large numbers of people at the least cost, that he contributes to progress by initiative and invention, and that he provides capital from which others benefit without taking any risk. I do not say that these claims are insincere or that they are not largely justified, but only that with the average business man they are his Sunday piety, largely ignored on weekdays. If his apology and his standards of practice coincided, there would be a notable alteration in his behavior.

The dictum "business is business" signifies that one is not expected in business to be governed, directly or indirectly, by benevolent motives. Business for personal profit becomes a refuge from morality, where success is applauded and not too closely scrutinized. The habits of mind developed in business cannot but be extended in some measure to the whole of the business man's life; and where, as in America, business is so highly honored, to the whole of society.

Political, legal, and economic *pursuits* tend to be deflected from the moral purpose for which these institutions exist. They tend to create non-moral attitudes and judgments in the most conspicuous and influential circles. To restore the moral meaning of these institutions, it is necessary to raise the level of the whole body of citizens. Somewhere, somehow, it is necessary to infuse the people at large with public spirit or social consciousness. It has been said that the comparative purity of political life in Great Britain has in the past been due in part to primogeniture. The younger sons, being obliged to seek a profession, went into public service and carried with them a code of high-minded principles deemed worthy of their noble origin. This is known as *noblesse oblige*. There is a noble origin which can be attributed to all American citizens, however—an inheritance of democratic citizenship, which should imply an honorable public responsibility.

In America, the ultimate cure for dishonesty or impropriety in office, for the willingness to connive at crime or suborn those in positions of trust, or for sharp practice in the great professions of politics, law, and business, can be found only in elevating the moral tone of the total society. This is the chief task of education, and its successful performance is the condition of the successful performance of all of education's other tasks. Education is here taken to include all the agencies, such as the home, the church, and all the agencies which employ the written or spoken word. It is peculiarly the duty of "formal" education; that is, of agencies designed expressly for educational purposes and owing allegiance to no other end. The hesitation of teachers to teach morality would be largely overcome if it were freed from any odor of sanctimoniousness, prudishness, or paternal admonition, and seen to be involved in every practical problem, as it is when reduced to its ultimate terms. Such morality is to be found not in the gallery but in the arena; not in the grandstand or bandstand, or on the sidelines, but on the field in the thick of the fray, where the work of the world is going on. Morality is both created and enacted by those who meet their fellow men in some field of action and discover the art of living peacefully and profitably together.

The family circle where parents meet children or each other, the conference where United Mine Workers meet coal operators, sittings of the N. A. A. C. P. where whites meet Negroes, the Congress where representatives meet representatives, the sessions of the Security Council where nation meets nation, are the seed beds of morality. These are the places where it grows, if at all. It will emerge only if the genius of harmony presides; but insofar as morality exists, this is where it comes into being—amidst difficulties, and with only occasional and partial triumphs. Insofar as the world grows morally better, here is the head of its advance. Here is the fighting front where every militant moralist will want to enlist for the duration.

CHAPTER IX

ARE WE AGAINST REVOLUTION?

The minds of Americans are now acutely troubled by "international problems." There is an historic irony, or perhaps retribution, in this. America was once regarded as a place of refuge from the chronic disturbances which afflicted less favored parts of the earth's surface; now there is no quarrel so slight or so remote that we do not feel concerned, or impelled to intervene. Americans once thought they could turn their backs on the rest of the world and devote themselves to their domestic fortunes, and to the perfection of their already almost perfect institutions. There were, of course, trade, Christian missions, and for the more privileged, travels abroad to observe with amused tolerance the strange behavior of foreigners. But their problems were not "our problems." Our duty toward them was felt to be discharged by setting them an example, and by permitting them, in diminishing numbers, to settle among us. Now they deposit their problems on our laps, and we feel, as the price of our power and prosperity, an obligation to solve them.

What are some of the more conspicuous features of this global situation in which we are called upon to assume so great a responsibility? In the forefront is the division of the world into two groups, one headed by Russia, the other by ourselves, which are profoundly suspicious of one another, arming against one another, and already far along on the road toward war. A hopeful view of this division of the world, and one which fifty years ago it was easy to take, is that a division of the world into two parts is the penultimate stage of the advance from plurality to unity. But there is another view: namely, that this is the penultimate stage of man's descent to self-destruction—because the belligerents are larger than ever before in history, and armed with more devastating weapons. It is the recognition and fear of this second alternative which gives the present situation its extreme gravity. We think of it not as an opportunity for good, but rather as an emergency in which we are called upon to save mankind from catastrophe.

Why is the world thus divided? I raise this question not for historical reasons but because diagnosis is the basis for prognosis and therapy. There are, of course, many reasons, as in all cases of historical explanation. But there is one general and fundamental reason for the present situation which lies in the background, and which has not, I believe, been sufficiently emphasized. I refer to the fact that different human societies do not develop simultaneously, and have difficulty, therefore, in understanding one another, and in working together.

We speak of the societies of Western Europe and North America as the relatively "advanced" societies, and we mean something quite specific by this, which may or may not coincide with one's ultimate scale of values. Thus, although some persons, inside and outside of India, would place Indian civilization above ours on the ground of its greater preoccupation with religion and the things of the spirit, no one would doubt that ours is the more advanced society. The accepted standards of advancement, or at least some of them, are technology, industrialization, material standard of living, education, public health, political autonomy and personal freedom. These are the criteria we have in mind when we speak of certain areas of the earth's surface as "backward" or "dependent" areas.

Judged by these standards, the human societies co-existing at any one time have reached different stages of advancement. Human progression in these respects is askew. Different societies do not advance abreast but in a staggered formation. This has been true in all periods of recorded history, and it is notably true at the present time. Advanced societies have advanced with unparalleled rapidity, while other societies have remained stationary or have been far outstripped.

Difference in stages of advancement determines the

relative capacity of societies to maintain certain forms of institutions, political, legal, economic, and cultural. It also determines the order of urgency—that is, what is deemed of immediate importance and what is postponed to the future. Thus, a society which is just emerging from primitivism will be obliged to develop its agricultural economy first, and postpone industrialization; food is its primary requirement, and may be the only product which it can hope to export in exchange for manufactured goods. Or, a society may be compelled to postpone industrialization until education has advanced to the point of developing certain skills and technologies; or it will have to postpone political autonomy until it has achieved a certain amount of experience in social organization and management. Personal freedom appears to be a late achievement, depending on many prior achievements, including a comparatively high standard of living.

It is customary to speak of "backward and dependent areas" as though there were two different kinds of areas, the "backward" and the "dependent." As a matter of fact they tend to be the same areas, for the backward become the dependent. The history of imperialism since the beginning of the great "voyages of discovery" in the fifteenth and sixteenth centuries has consisted mainly of the conquest and exploitation of the backward areas of the Far East, Africa, and the Americas by the advanced nations of Europe.

Economic and political imperialism marched hand in hand. The other half, the backward and dependent half of imperialism, is referred to as "colonialism," but should be taken to include lesser degrees of dependence, such as "protectorates."

At any given time, then, the various groups of mankind will have reached different stations on the journey of civilization, and their outlooks and pressing concerns will be different. This would not have disturbed the general peace of the world if these groups had remained isolated, or if the backward groups had remained so backward as to be unable to resist the aggression of the advanced. But in recent years the backward have learned and borrowed from the advanced. There is a circle in imperialism. The imperial powers, in order to profit by their imperialism, have been impelled to raise standards of living in their dependencies, and to introduce among them the very arts for lack of which they had become dependent.

And now all parts of the world are brought into close relations by communication and interaction. The achievements of the more advanced societies are promptly and widely known to the less advanced, which become discontented. The backward insist on coming forward, and the dependent insist on independence. And they demand that these changes shall take place at once, rejecting the proverb, "Rome was not built in a day." Nor can it be proved that in this they are mistaken; perhaps in modern times Rome *could* be built in a day. And from the different stages of advancement and dependence there spring misunderstandings and conflicting conceptions of world order. Each society seeks to save itself, other societies, and the world at large, by its own social gospel.

At the same time that backward and dependent societies are on the move, so within each society the relatively backward and dependent classes are also pressing forward. Throughout their entire history, the masses of mankind have worked with their hands, whether as peasants or as industrial workers. They have worked for bare subsistence, and in dependence on landed proprietors or capitalistic employers. These masses have now acquired both the idea and the means of improving their condition.

These two revolutions, the external and the internal, the one directed against the imperialistic invader and the other against the agricultural or industrial overlord, feel a community of interest and have formed a partnership. This consolidated revolutionary movement is something new in the world. The great revolutions of the past, which Americans accept as milestones of progress and as a part of their own "glorious" tradition—the English Revolution of 1688, the American Revolutions, North and South, the French Revolution—were revolutions of one middle-class or advanced society against another.

There have, in the past, been pitiful slave insurrections, helots' and peasants' rebellions, gallant last stands of American, Asiatic, and African natives against European conquerors carrying superior weapons. But today for the first time aborigines and proletariat are equipped and organized; moved by common grievances of the past and common hopes of the future; led by agitators who know how to excite both of these emotions; and thus enabled to take advantage of their numbers and meet on equal terms or better those whom they consider their oppressors.

A world so various in its stages of social development, so permeated with conflicting forces, and nevertheless so interconnected part with part that the safety and prosperity of each depends on the safety and prosperity of all—this world is at the present time drawn to two opposite focal centers of power and appeal: the one is Russian in power and Communistic in appeal; the other is American in power and individualistic-democratic in appeal. Power is ranged against power, and appeal bids against appeal for the support of mankind at large. This is the "cold war" which has prevented the United Nations from fulfilling its purpose and has created a threat of universal war at the very time when the hopes of man were set on universal and lasting peace. But whether there be cold war, or hot war, or peaceful rivalry, the victory will lie with that group of nations which wins the sympathy and support of the masses of mankind that are now stirred by the revolutionary impulse.

Owen Lattimore, having in mind conditions in the Far East, has said: "Unless we can learn to match the Russians in professional skill in the art of influencing revolutions which we cannot control, the advantage will lie with them." [1] The most significant part of this observation lies in the words "which we cannot control." The revolutions of today are not created from the outside by propaganda or infiltration, but spring from within. They would occur if there were no interference. But when they are thus accepted as forces which cannot be prevented or stopped, they can be "influenced" from abroad by those who win the confidence of their leaders.

It is a flagrant fact that Communism makes a strong appeal to the revolutionary movement. It promises immediate action, and has proved its words by deeds, both in Russia herself and in other countries which have been converted to Communism and follow her lead. The action of Communism, in its first phase, coincides precisely with the existing revolutionary impulse, both internal and external. It confiscates the estates of the great landowners and divides them among land-hungry peasants; it destroys the wealth of capitalistic *entrepreneurs* and exalts the resentful worker above them in social esteem. It declares its hostility to the great imperialistic powers of the nineteenth century, and supports every uprising of their colonies and dependencies. Owing to her own revolutionary experience, Russia can export advisers trained in the techniques of revolution, as America exports engineers or missionaries. Russia boldly avows this pro-revolutionary policy, spreads it abroad, and pursues it with a relentlessness, promptness, and single-mindedness that are made possible by her highly centralized political control.

In this rivalry of appeal to the revolutionary world, America suffers from the defects of her merits. A democracy which is wavering and discordant at home can scarcely speak with firmness and consistency abroad. A democracy in which every policy, foreign and domestic, must be debated at length before it can be adopted and executed, cannot act promptly. When it does act promptly, as in Korea, it is afterward overtaken with doubts and sometimes reverses itself. It is inhibited by scruples. Its own idea of revolution is opposed to the use of force, and is both less dramatic and less congenial to people who are already inflamed and impatient.

Our advantage lies in the superiority of our *idea* of revolution. We are not against revolution, if by revolution is meant change, even radical change, in the direction of the rise of the masses to greater independence and higher standards of living. We are against violent revolution, believing that the loss outweighs the gain. We have had abundant opportunity to observe chronic revolution among our neighbors to the South. The Bolshevik Revolution of 1917 was a bloody revolution, the costs of which have not yet been paid; and this is the kind of revolution which Soviet Russia foments and abets throughout the world, and to which she looks for the salvation of mankind. She has come by this idea honestly—that is to say, it is written in her Book. It is her orthodox economic and political gospel. Russia is committed by her Communist creed to the doctrine that the conflict between the bourgeoisie and the proletariat, and between the imperial power and the dependency, are irreconcilable conflicts, because those who hold the advantage cannot be persuaded to yield it—it has to be taken away from them, and they must be annihilated lest they seek to recover it. This doctrine is based partly on Marxist dogma, partly on Russian experience, and partly on wishful thinking—the Communists hope to profit by disorder.

There is abundant evidence that the idea of violent revolution is an essential part of Soviet policy. Thus Vaclav Kopecky, Minister of Information in Czechoslovakia, is quoted as saying of a "treasonable conspiracy" that "the plot had started because many Communists lacked vigilance and failed to understand that socialism in this country was neither gradualist nor nationalist, but was based on Soviet help." [2] In other words, the Soviet revolutionary policy is opposed to a gradual reform moving toward their avowed socialist end, and favors the kind

of abrupt change that is brought about by plot, resisted by counterplot, and directed from the Kremlin.

The Western world has become suspicious of violent revolution on general grounds. Such revolutions
appear to follow a cycle: "the honeymoon," "the rule
of the moderate," "the accession of extremists," "reigns
of terror," a period of convalescence and finally, dictatorship.[3] The tempo and steps need not be the
same, but the broad line remains the same—from an
old oppression to a new, through an intervening period of civil war. Violence makes enemies who look
for the time of reprisal; the fear of such reprisals
hardens the revolutionary leadership, which, having
used dictatorial power to overthrow and repress its
internal enemies, retains it as a habit and vested interest. There is no régime more hostile to revolution
than a régime established by revolution. The revolutionary conspiracy which seizes power, employs a
secret police to perpetuate it.

The United States of America sprang from a political, and not from a social revolution. In fact, the
American Revolution is now described not as a revolution at all, but as a "war for independence." Its
enemy was external rather than internal and America was then largely spared the pains of a struggle
between class and class. Even the Civil War is now
by preference called a "war between the states." The
right of revolution was justified in theory by the doctrine of the Declaration of Independence and by its

author, Thomas Jefferson. Americans have been quick to sympathize with political revolutions outside their border. But they have grown increasingly sceptical even of political revolutions, and, in view of the havoc which it wrought, they now think remorsefully even of the Civil War, and like to speculate on the possibility that the Union might have been saved, and slavery abolished, by peaceful means.

The Soviet idea is that in human progress it is necessary that things grow worse before they can be better, and that constructive change can be achieved only by destruction. The opposite idea, now known as "gradualism," means that grievances shall be removed *before* they break into violence. The French Revolution, the Chinese Revolution, and the Russian Revolution itself, were long in coming, and their violence and destructiveness were proportional to the time in which they had gathered force. History records the fact that grievances are long remembered, and that if they are not promptly satisfied they will fester and corrupt. People cherish them and professional agitators excite them. Even when they are eventually successful, the hatred which inspired them remains an obsession long after its occasion has been removed. Taking account of the immediate evils of violent revolution, the relapses which follow, and the scars that remain, Americans look for another way of dealing with oppression and reaction.

Gradualism is based on the belief that what is

[156]

better in the new can be achieved without the destruction of what is good in the old. Although this belief is founded largely on faith, it is a faith which has been proved. The biographer of Florence Nightingale draws us two pictures of life in England in 1842. The first depicts a house party given at Chatsworth by the Duke of Devonshire, in honor of H.R.H. the Duke of Sussex:

All the society of the north assembled, and in honor of the Royal guest the huge house was crammed with "Howards, Cavendishes, Percys, Greys, all in gala dress with stars, garters, diamonds and velvets" . . . The entertainment was planned on an enormous scale. . . . (The) head gardener . . . had erected a vast glasshouse in the Park, "An omnibus . . . plied at the gates . . . every evening to take those who could not walk so far to the monster conservatory, which covers an acre of ground, and where groves of palms and bananas are making all haste to grow to their natural size," etc, etc.

Here is the other picture:

Eighteen forty-two was a terrible year for the people of England. The country was in the grip of what has passed into history as "the hungry forties." In villages, as in towns, there were starvation, sweated labor, ignorance and dirt. Diseased scarecrows swarmed not only in the airless undrained courts of London, but in the "black filth" of rural cottages; workhouses, hospitals and prisons were overflowing. . . . Florence wrote in a private note: "My mind is absorbed with the idea of the sufferings of man, it besets me behind and before. . . . All the people I see are eaten up with care or poverty or disease." [4]

[*157*]

These extremes of luxury and misery existed side by side in England. But such contrasts could be found in America as well, during the decades that followed. It is revolting to the modern conscience that they should have ever existed. There is no condoning of past evil, however, in pointing out that such evils have been continuously diminished. Both countries have experienced the gross abuses of the Industrial Revolution and have in large measure corrected them. Both countries have witnessed the growing power of organized labor. Both countries have witnessed the growing equality of wealth and opportunity. The contrast between 1842 and 1951 in both countries is scarcely less striking than that between the two contemporary sides of English life in 1842.

This change has taken a century—much too long, no doubt—but it has been accomplished without a war of class against class, without a plundering of the rich by the poor, and without a breach in the continuity of political institutions. There has been no "liquidation" of the already privileged in order that the masses of the people might obtain new privileges. Since there has been no violent revolution, there has been no counter-revolution. There is no legacy of hate and fear of reprisals. Both countries have grown into something better without having to be killed and then born again.

Gradualism has its pitfalls. The counsel to "make haste slowly" is often a pretext for not advancing at all. If gradual reform is to satisfy grievances, it must not be too gradual. It must be visible to the naked eye. It must be timed to meet the natural impatience of those who would like to see a difference while they are still around to enjoy it. To those who live in 1950, pie in the year 2000 is not much better than "pie in the sky by-and-by."

Gradualism not only should, but tends to be, accelerated. Luxury and misery can no longer dwell side by side without being aware of one another. Gross inequalities cannot be hidden. Man's humane impulses are increasingly evoked, and provided with more occasions on which to express themselves. Social remedies have been found, and as reform succeeds, old habits are broken and new adjustments are easier to make.

It will be objected that this is too rosy a picture. But it is not untrue to history. It does not imply that the road ahead is not long and difficult to travel. And what there is in it of faith is the vital faith of Americans. The old creed must find new applications under changed conditions, but we were from the beginning committed to novelty and change. We pledged ourselves to social progress as a perpetual endeavor, and promised to extend its benefits to ever-widening circles. As a people who fought for independence against a mighty empire at the height of its power, political self-determination has been with us an instinctive belief. As the fortunate possessors of a land greatly favored by nature, we have from the beginning felt that that land and its resources were held in trust for *all* of our people in order that they might *all* enjoy an increasing abundance of life. Where we have failed we have failed with an uneasy conscience, and with the sense of a task unfulfilled.

We are, then, the natural allies of that double revolution which disturbs the world today. Because that revolution also receives friendly overtures from Communism, we are obliged to prove that we are its *better* friends. In various parts of the world we have been compelled to choose between avowed enemies of revolution and those whom we regard as its false friends. In confused situations, where issues were mixed and lines were crossed, we have chosen evil because we thought it to be the lesser evil. We have made unholy alliances. Because we believe them to be dominated by a Communist leadership which will eventually betray them, we find ourselves in the Philippines assisting in the annihilation of Hukbalahap, which is the remnant of the hard core of resistance to Japanese occupation, and is made up largely of exploited and landless peasants.

This situation has repeated itself in various parts of the world. We have been too ready to side with law and order, or to yield to immediate expediency. We have too readily allied ourselves with the allies of those who are engaged in suppressing that very revolution of which we are the professed friends.

But it is not too late to mend, and until we do we cannot either be faithful to ourselves or assume that rôle of moral leadership to which the world has summoned us.

CHAPTER X

WHAT PRICE WAR?

War is at once the most natural thing in the world and the most absurd.[1] It is natural because man is something of a predatory animal. He is carnivorous and not herbivorous despite the gospel of the vegetarians; he eats other animals, and was a hunter before he acquired the arts of agriculture. He does not often eat his fellowmen (though he sometimes does), but he readily becomes a cannibal in other ways, as in rape or pillage. He finds it natural to use other men to satisfy his appetites.

This might be called unilateral war—when the other man cannot or does not fight back. Bilateral war is also natural. When different men or groups of men both want what they cannot both have, they quarrel; and when they quarrel, they warm up to it. They call into play a combative drive which nature has provided for such situations: and when this enters, it is likely to take possession. The desire to hurt and kill then takes the place of the original desire to possess. When men for any reason are especially quarrelsome in mood or character, the fire is easily kindled and quickly spread.

Since war is a bilateral affair, it may be caused by fear; that is, by the expectation of injury from another. This is known as "preventive war," in which one side takes the advantage of striking the first blow. When fear and suspicion are for any reason spread and intensified, they create a highly combustible situation in which war may be started by a trivial incident or by misunderstanding another's intentions. Since it is characteristic of men that they have families, friends, and partners, they reckon the enemies of these others as their own. Moreover, through pride or honor, men feel that a fight once undertaken must be a fight to the finish—once committed, they must expend their full force to destroy the enemy. Thus, a slight offense may cause a holocaust. In short, war is natural and human, all too human.

Things are not inevitable because they are natural. That the natural is not the inevitable might be said to be the very principle of human life—that is to say, of *human* life. Men have not only instincts, but also faculties of thought and choice—also provided by nature, and sometimes called "higher" nature. Whatever raw nature may impel men to do, they can learn to do better by experience, and to govern their action by ideas. This is sometimes called "acquired" nature. To consider war inevitable because it is natural is a surrender and betrayal of man's claim to be something more than animal. Not long ago the following paragraph appeared in an American newspaper—in a column entitled "The Lighter Side"(!):

It makes me sick, way down deep to read about Senators who want to support China with money. There is only one way to chase the Reds out of China, only one way to lick them, and that is to send 30 or 40 divisions of troops, supported by everything we have—tanks, planes, artillery, etc. But that means war. It sure does. War with all its horror, with all its misery and all its heartaches. . . . Heaven knows I don't want another war, if there were any way to avoid it. But the world today is A against B. A thinks this way and B thinks another. Just as sure as I am sitting here at this type-writer, A and B are going to clash. They'll find one another. Bound to.[2]

This "I don't want another war, *but*," this regret that does nothing about it, this acceptance of the inevitable, this laying of the burden in the lap of nature and destiny, is modern man's way of sparing himself the pains of intellectual and moral effort.

Raw nature is also on the other side; peace, too, is natural and human. Men can sometimes have what they desire without taking it away from others. They like to share things, and they even like one another. There is a blessedness in giving as well as in receiving. Nature has equipped men for living peacefully together by implanting the parental and filial instincts in them, plus a general disposition of fellow-feeling. This does not make peace, any more than war, inevitable.

In short, man is a fighting animal, and he is also a loving animal; so far as the animal in him goes, he may be either. And so far as *human* nature goes, he may be either. For his faculties of thought and choice may be harnessed to either set of impulses. A rational war is much more devastating than a dog fight. But whether man goes to war or lives at peace falls within that province of his life which is not left to his sheer impulses. He organizes war and he organizes peace, and which shall be subordinated to the other depends on how he organizes his life as a whole. Man is a self-justifying being who seeks reasons for what he does, and does that for which he finds reasons, whether it be war or peace.

How, then, can he justify war? When this question is put in general terms, the answer is easy—the difficulty lies in the application to a particular situation. Since war is evidently destructive, consisting as it does in killing and wounding, in committing wholesale every crime of which man is capable, and in ruining the laboriously accumulated products of his toil, there is a strong presumption against it. Indeed, the presumption is so strong that there are some who take the position that war is *never* justified.

There are, however, grounds on which war, despite its evils, is acceptable as the lesser of evils. The glamour of war is a thing of the past. The word "warrior" is obsolete, as signifying an honorable vocation in which one brave and skillful man of arms wagers his life against that of another, for glory or for country. War has its incidents of heroism, especially on the lower levels of rank; but taken as a whole it has assumed the form of a cold-blooded and systematic destruction from which unarmed civilians and armed soldiers suffer alike. And war has lost its glamorous appeal because men are now aware of its grim realities. The record of war is no longer written by poets, but by its disillusioned victims. But even so there are grounds on which war is acceptable as a painful necessity. The first of these grounds is bodily self-preservation. He who takes life takes all. If war is detested because it destroys life, then life is accounted good or the bearer of good. He who rejects war because it destroys civilization must face the fact that civilization can also be destroyed, and destroyed finally, by the killing of civilized men. So long as men live there is always the possibility that civilization may be restored; but if their lives are destroyed even this possibility is removed.

The same is to be said of subjection. He who destroys freedom destroys all. What is accounted good in life is realized through choice, and he whose will is broken ceases to be an instrument of good. In short, he who fights for life and for freedom is fighting for all those hopes and aspirations which underlie his rejection of war. He is seeking to avoid a condition of mankind in which there is nobody left but dead men, slaves, and evil-doers.

This is the same as to say that war is justified when it is defensive, but not when it is offensive. No doubt offensive war may be disguised as defensive war. No doubt the offensive may *become* defensive through the counter-attack of the opponent. But there *is* a war-making which is defensive, namely, when it originates in the offensive of the opponent. And this cannot always be avoided since its avoidance would require a control of the other party's action and intention. This is sometimes expressed by saying that it takes only one to start a war, but takes two to prevent or stop it.

Under modern conditions of war, the resort to war is justified only as a *last* resort. Its unprecedented destructiveness to all parties, offensive and defensive alike, implies that there shall be a sureness, correspondingly great, that life and freedom are really at stake.

War is not inevitable, nor is it always avoidable. Since it is, under certain circumstances, justifiable, preparation for it is also justifiable. Modern war, even if defensive, cannot be hastily improvised with any hope of success; and without hope of success it ceases to be justifiable. Weapons, mobilization and training have to be planned on a scale, and with a degree of efficiency, corresponding to those of the potential enemy. By the same token defensive alliances, treaties, and pacts are justifiable. But at the same time that one prepares for war because it is possible though

[*167*]

regrettable, one aims at peace because it is both possible and desirable.

Peace needs no argument beyond a recapitulation of the evils of war. In seeking peace, we seek to avoid the immediate evils of violence—loss of life, wounds and mutilation, ruin of property, all the degradations and bestialities resulting from the breaking down of normal restraints. At the same time we seek to avoid the costs of mobilization: the loss of time, the diverting of production to useless uses, the waste of resources, the burden of taxation, the terrible boredom and obsessions, the mental and spiritual impoverishments of military life. I shall not attempt to portray the horrors of a Third World War, implemented by atomic, and perhaps bio-logical, weapons. The horrors of such a war, which no one could hope to escape, have been portrayed by many writers—from the cool calculations of the scientists to the lurid imaginings of Aldous Huxley. Nothing that I could say would add to the vividness of the picture, though attention should be called to the quickness with which people forget such lessons and fall to playing with fire.

To these evils are to be added the more indirect, but deeper and more lasting, effects upon the mind and soul. In World War II, an American soldier had been wounded and captured in North Africa and put in a German hospital, where he remained until the Tunis surrender; whereupon the *Herrenvolk* came and surrendered to him, much to his embarrassment. He summed up this experience to the American doctor by saying, "Except when I see him over the sights of my gun, Jerry is good enough for me." [3]

It is a bad thing to see a fellow human being over the sights of a gun. He ceases to be a human being, and becomes an enemy, intent on killing you unless you kill him first. War obliterates not only the human qualities which evoke the natural instinct of fellow-feeling, but also the qualities by which one nation or individual may hope to surpass another. Men of every race, creed and culture tend to be reduced to interchangeable parts of a military machine. All armies, navies, and forces use the same techniques, and even the same discipline and "tables of organization." Men do not merely *use* standardized weapons, they *become* standardized weapons.

War imposes its own necessities, which violate the very principles for which men fight, or for which, in a democratic country, they are taught to believe they fight. Men fight for peace, but they *make* war. They fight for their homes, but for months and years they leave their homes, and may through absence destroy them. They fight for individual freedom but they surrender their individual freedom to a line of command. They fight for the Christian gospel of love, but in war they learn to hate.

On the side of peace, we must reckon not only the avoidance of war's depravities, but all positive benefits as well. Peace is not merely the absence of war, but the presence of all the good things of life and the hopes of better things to come. It is this infinite fruitfulness of peace, and of the security of a permanent peace, that sets it above every other earthly goal.

Man's hope of permanent peace depends on extending to all international relations the same methods of reconciling conflicting interests that have achieved peace in varying degrees all along the line, from the individual person to limited groups of nations that have become friendly allies. This is the purpose of the United Nations, or of whatever better union may be put in its place. Security is the product of agreement, together with the added sanction of a collective force to prevent breaches of this agreement by any of the contracting parties. While it is true that collective security has not yet been attained, it would be premature to say that it has permanently failed. It remains not only as a hope, but as a necessity.

The basis of collective security on the global scale, as on any lesser scale, is moral and not coercive. It requires a will to agree, which must be converted into dispositions and habits. International agreement is as yet in an unfinished stage, half-built, half-blueprint, loosely basted or tacked together. To become a firm and lasting structure, it requires an international-mindedness similar to that narrower loyalty which now binds the members of a nation. It is not sufficient that governments should make treaties of expediency; it is necessary that peoples should feel themselves to be fellow-members of this greater community. The development of this will and sentiment to the point at which it becomes the inheritance of each successive generation is a task of education—of moral education.

Meanwhile Americans must pursue peace while at the same time they take precautions against the possibility of war. This balance of purpose and prudence is not easily achieved. One thing is clear: namely, that the best assurance of peace is to cling to what peace we have, so long as we have it. Instruments of war must be prepared, but the dominant pattern of our behavior must be peaceful. In proportion as we feel and act *as if* we were at war, we approach and even at moments cross that line which still divides us from actually *being* at war.

At the present moment the possible war and the peace which we pursue lie between ourselves and Soviet Russia. Our fear of war from Soviet Russia is not a groundless fear, and preparation to meet it is not unreasonable. The grounds of our fear are many, and we are so often reminded of them that they need only the briefest mention here. The chief of these grounds is the possibility that desire for peace and counsels of prudence may be outweighed by fanaticism. The fanaticism of Soviet Russia, like most fanaticisms, rests on historical determinism. Convinced Communists believe that their triumph is predetermined, and that they are the instruments of destiny. It is this which accounts for their inhumanity and unscrupulousness. The Cause is greater than any man or group of men; it is a Moloch to which human sacrifices are willingly, joyfully, made. Convinced as they are that the salvation of mankind lies in the triumph of this Cause, Communists are disposed to impose it on the world.

To remove this disposition there is little we can do. But there is a second ground of fear which is within our control. This is the vicious circle of fear. We have reason to fear that Soviet Russia, judging by our behavior, has reason to fear our warlike intentions. If this circle is to be broken, it is our concern to break it where it passes through ourselves.

There are certain ways you behave when you are at war, and certain other ways you behave when you are still at peace and are still hoping to preserve peace. We are behaving, at least a highly vociferous and audible part of us, as though we were committed to war—as though the die were cast.

Thus, when you are at war you treat a certain other nation as an enemy. You call him by bad names, you exhaust your vocabulary of abuse, assuming that friendly words or gestures are now out of order, since they can only weaken your will to war. You attempt to out-Vishinsky Vishinsky. If you are at war, it is excusable that your Chief of Staff, even if he be as admirable as General Bradley, should liken the rival nation to a "jackal denied his plunder." [4] If you are at war, you will applaud when a distinguished visiting statesman and master of rhetoric expresses regret that the opponent was not "strangled at his birth"; or when he likens him to some notoriously hateful enemy of the past, such as "the Mongol." [5] You are aware that such statements are going to intensify your enemy's hostility, but this does not disturb you when you have abandoned any thought of peace.

If you are at war, you view the words and professions of your enemy with suspicion. If he makes friendly gestures, you assume that he doesn't mean them. If he speaks of peace, you call it a "peace offensive." You assume that it can only be intended to catch you off your guard, and weaken your will to destroy him. If he proposes that the heads of state meet to attempt some sort of reconciliation, you scornfully reject the proposal.* If he proposes that

*The Richmond *Times Dispatch* of April 10, 1948, published an article based on previous articles in *Business Week* and the *United States News,* to the effect that President Truman had "rebuffed the suggestion" of two such meetings. One of the alleged proposals was for a meeting between President Truman and Premier Stalin in Stockholm, and the proposal is said to have been made about a month before the seizure of Czechoslovakia, and to have had something to do with the more aggressive turn of Soviet policy.

both parties put aside their weapons, you assume that that is only so that he can take advantage of your weakness.

You do to him the things which you complain of his doing to you. Thus, having accused him of hiding himself behind an "iron curtain," and of refusing to allow his citizens to go abroad lest they see how much better our way of life is than his, then, when, at the invitation of some of your own people, he sends a group of musicians, writers, and scientists to visit you, you snub them and accuse them of being spies. If he repatriates German war prisoners, as you have complained of his *not* doing, you then complain that they are "well-fed and well-clothed," and that, having been indoctrinated, they will help to win over their German compatriots to the Russian side.[6] Nothing that he does is right.

All of this makes sense if you are engaged in a fighting war. It is not in itself precisely reasonable, but then unreason is characteristic of war, once the fighting has begun. If, however, you have not decided upon war, if you are still hoping and striving for peace, then warlike behavior does *not* make sense. If you have peace, and are still trying to keep it, then the reasonable thing is not to treat the other party as an enemy, but as a friend; or if not as a friend, then as a possible friend; or if not as a possible friend, then at least as a neighbor.

If this is your purpose, and so long as it is your

purpose, you avoid words and deeds that will make such neighborliness impossible. If the other party makes an offer to negotiate, you accept it, not because you are confident of the outcome, but because it is sufficient that a successful outcome should be barely possible. You leave no stone unturned to find an agreement, even a temporary agreement, which will give time for the sharp edges of acrimony to be dulled. If the other party sends emissaries, private or official, you receive them with at least formal courtesy and do not prejudge their motives. As regards the other party's motives, you give him the benefit of the doubt. There is then an immense good to be gained if you are proved right; while if you are proved wrong, there is little to lose, and you will at least have kept your own record clear.

You exercise yourself occasionally in the art of seeing the other man's point of view. You don't adopt it, but you imagine it, so that you can understand it better and not attribute it merely to malice and low cunning. You show forbearance even when the other party does not, for there is more at stake than scoring at repartee.

You take what immediate steps you can that look toward a permanent peace. You may believe that World Government provides the only permanent escape from the menace of war; and with that ulterior end in view, you work with the Charter of the United Nations. Finding that the United Nations does not work because there is a feud between two groups of nations, you attack that feud, and try to remove its causes. You play for time, and persist in your efforts, not for five years, but, if necessary, for ten years or *more*. You show patience and persistence —pursuing your end for as long as may be necessary; for you know that if you abandon it now, you will be compelled to resume it at some later time.

In his famous Address to the Joint Meeting of Congress, on April 19, 1951, General MacArthur said:

Military alliances, balances of power, leagues of nations, all in turn failed, leaving the only path to be by way of the crucible of war. The utter destructiveness of war now blocks out this alternative. We have had our last chance. If we will not devise some greater and more equitable system, our Armageddon will be at our door. The problem basically is theological and involves a spiritual recrudescence, an improvement of human character that will synchronize with our almost matchless advances in science, art, literature and all material and cultural developments of the past 2000 years. It must be of the spirit if we are to save the flesh.

But once [war is] forced upon us, there is no other alternative than to apply every available means to bring it to a swift end. War's very object is victory, not prolonged indecision.

In war there is no substitute for victory.[7]

General MacArthur's address made plain the soundness of the American subordination of the military to the civilian authority, and the ground for

[*176*]

his own removal. Because the military authority is assigned the limited task of military victory, it must be over-ruled, if necessary, by the political authority which assumes responsibility for the larger and ultimate victory. A military victory *may*, in this larger and ultimate sense, be a defeat. Whether it shall be war or withdrawal, total war or limited war, stalemate or a war to a finish, is to be decided on other than military grounds and by the makers of policy rather than by its instruments.

The fitting of the short-range to the long-range, and of the part to the whole, calls for a total foreign policy, animated by the purpose of reconciling peace with survival and freedom. This purpose is not the exclusive purpose of any single party, left or right, but of the nation guided by its responsible statesmen and supported by the will of all the people.

CHAPTER XI

TOTAL FOREIGN POLICY

The proof of the citizen's capacity to decide is to *decide*—here and now, amidst all the perplexities which beset him. While he may not claim finality or infallibility, he may nevertheless be prepared to say, "This is what I think, as of today, and subject to correction." And the best proof that his decision is a thoughtful decision, and not a snap judgment or mere echo, will be his taking the long and total, and not merely the short and partial, view of public policy.

A foreign correspondent of the *New York Times*, writing from Paris on October 19, 1949, quotes what he called a "pellucid summary of the United States' foreign policy" which he had obtained from "an important United States statesman who has much to do with the shaping of this policy." The summary ran, in part, as follows:

United States foreign policy is the sum total of the aspirations and reactions of the American people, with relation to world affairs, as they are channeled up through the executive branch of the Government and through Congress. . . .

The objective of American foreign policy is to create a stable, orderly and peaceful world in which all nations— the United States in particular—are making their own special contribution to prosperity and to the international community.

Because of its summary character, this admirable statement makes a distinction which it does not altogether clarify. The "aspirations and reactions of the American people with relation to world affairs" include many ideas on which Americans differ from one another and from the people of other friendly nations. These fall within that "special contribution" which a "stable, orderly and peaceful world" will enable us to make. The most notable example is religion. Christianity is one of the "aspirations and reactions" of the American people, but so are other religions, or substitutes for religion. It is not an objective of *foreign policy* to convert the world to Christianity, but to bring about a world in which this particular "aspiration and reaction" can be "contributed" in peaceful association or rivalry with other beliefs.

This is a distinction of no small importance in the present situation. Capitalism, for example, is one of our aspirations, and in a "stable, orderly and peaceful world' it will have its chance along with other forms of economy. It is no part of our foreign policy to promote capitalism any more than Christianity, or modern art, or the theory of relativity, or the con-

sumption of Coca-Cola. In a wholesale indictment
of Communism this distinction is overlooked. Our
foreign policy is directed against Communism taken
as the enemy of a "stable, orderly and peaceful
world," not against Communism taken as atheism
or socialism.

There is only one phase of our foreign policy in
which possible exception can be taken to this distinction; namely, propaganda. When we present our
claims to leadership it is proper that we should include our culture, and not merely our championship
of peace. But even here pains should be taken to
emphasize its total richness and diversity rather than
any part on which we are divided, or which divides
us from the other cultures of mankind. For we desire
to unite Americans and non-Americans of diverse
cultural creeds on the fundamental purpose of creating a world in which there is room for all. Our
desire is to bring them all in. The adherent of any
one of these creeds may then legitimately hope that,
given freedom for all, his own will triumph by persuasion.

American foreign policy as defined above implies
that it should be closely bound to the United Nations, which is its best, and it might be said, its only
present hope of success. The deep disappointment at
the failure of the United Nations to fulfill expectations
proves how high and how imperative these expectations are. But it has a record of achievement in the

Near East and elsewhere, and in economic and cultural, as well as in political fields. If it is abandoned now it will have to be done over again. The very fact that it is an arena of dispute, where differences are aired, and where words are exchanged instead of blows, is of high importance. Discussion is in itself a kind of agreement, on which all other agreements must be built.

The so-called "crisis," "emergency," or "present danger" which calls for immediate action and self-sacrifice is only a phase of a troubled state that is likely to last for many years. There is an acute malady and there is a chronic malady, and the remedies used to cure the one must not be allowed to aggravate the other. Short-term and long-term thinking must be carried on together. And the forces which are at work in the world, the forces which we fear or with which we must deal and come to terms, must be met on many fronts. We must be politic and diplomatic; we must be prepared to repel violence with violence; we must explain ourselves to the world so that we can keep our old friends and, if possible, make new ones; we must help other peoples to help themselves and to help us. All of these things are necessary, war or no war—to avert war, to win war, to put things together again after war, to go on living with confidence and hopefulness in the absence of war.

Foreign policy, then, has four fronts: diplomacy

and politics, armament, propaganda, and world development. None of these can be neglected, and as tactical parts of a total strategy, each must be coördinated with the rest.

Diplomacy is not what it used to be. It was once a negotiation carried on diplomatically by diplomats, in secret, or at least in private. Now it is "open," and therefore exposed to the surrounding currents of popular emotion and opinion. The diplomat has to face two ways: toward his antagonist, and toward his own people. This considerably limits his freedom of action. He might, if it were left to him, make concessions to the antagonist abroad when he dare not do so under the eye of the people at home.

The recent negotiations over Germany prove how difficult it is for diplomats to carry on cool discussion at the same time that people are emotionally inflamed. A disinterested American observer described one of the days of the Paris meeting of deputies as consisting of "obstinate exchanges of diatribes." This applied apparently to Dr. Jessup, Mr. Davies, and M. Parodi, as well as to Mr. Gromyko, except that the first three all took Mr. Gromyko on in rotation. Who can say whether this manner and attitude on the part of our diplomatic representatives reflected the irate temper of the American people, or set an example which the American people imitated. In any case, it is bad for home consumption, and it is difficult to see what useful purpose it can serve abroad.

It is a peculiarly poor method of avoiding war, since it intensifies old enmities and makes no new friends.

There is no reason to believe that the maxims of good diplomacy are essentially different from those which govern successful private relations: *When you accuse an opponent of bad manners, don't imitate them. Don't become heated* (indignation is often a fine thing, but not in diplomats—that's not what we have them for). *If, being exasperated by the annoying behavior of your opponent, you find your nerves wearing thin, retire for a time until you have recovered your composure, and, if possible, your sense of humor* (perhaps our diplomats should employ the "platoon" system of football, and from time to time send in a fresh team). *Don't scold, denounce, stigmatize, castigate, insinuate, brand, or threaten* (these only beget a response in kind). *Don't boast* (it may save explanations later). *Don't make mortal enemies* (you may need them some day as friends). *Don't hate* (it is bad for mental and physical hygiene, as well as for morals). *Never use the word "never"* (you may want to change your mind). *Try to understand the opponent's point of view* (it will help you to deal with him).

International diplomacy consists essentially in the seeking of agreement by exchange of concessions. It is as important to be willing to make them, as it is to ask them. Above all it is important to renounce the primitive satisfaction of humiliating the oppon-

[*183*]

ent. When "face" becomes involved, the merits of the original question become subordinated to fictitious and (in the light of history) trivial values.

The point at which the opponent shows signs of making what you deem the essential concessions is the time to relax the pressure lest you drive him to the last desperate measure of pride. In February, 1865, President Lincoln proposed to his cabinet that $400,000,000 be appropriated to compensate the former slaveholders and to rehabilitate the South. To posterity, having in mind the dreadful aftermath of the Reconstruction, this sounds like high-minded statesmanship. The following is quoted from Carl Sandburg's account of the episode:

Welles in his diary sketched it as a scheme which he (Lincoln) hoped would be successful in promoting peace. . . . It did not meet with favor, but was dropped. "The earnest desire of the President to conciliate and effect peace was manifest, but there may be such a thing as so overdoing as to cause a distrust or adverse feeling." In the present temper of Congress, judged Welles, "the proposed measure, if a wise one, could not be carried through successfully. . . . The Rebels would misconstrue it if the offer were made." Usher wrote of the President [as] somewhat surprised at all the Cabinet being opposed. . . . With a deep sigh . . . [Lincoln] added, "But you are all opposed to me, and I will not send the message." [1]

The eloquence of Lincoln's sigh has, I believe, some bearing on events and attitudes in Korea and Washington.

When we turn to the political aspects of our foreign policy, it is comparatively easy to find fault with what is done in a time when nothing that is done can be right. The fundamental causes of the crisis were beyond the control of the United States. Our public officials have been obliged to make the best of a bad situation, and even the best made of a bad situation is not likely to be very good. It is also comparatively easy for "Monday morning quarterbacks," who were not calling the signals at the time, to pick flaws in past decisions. The opposition political party makes the most of these advantages, and adds the further complaint that the Government has consisted of Democrats, who therefore suffered in an extraordinary degree from human incapacity.

When the leaders of the opposition offer constructive proposals of their own, they are not impressive. Although they proclaim a policy of withdrawal in Europe they betray a suspicious interest in Formosa, which is even further away. They seem disposed to believe that Chiang Kai-shek, who could not stay on the mainland when he was there, can conquer it from outside; and that if he did do so he would bring the Chinese people "liberty"—especially if the United States were to assist by blowing up or starving a few hundreds of thousands of the enslaved Chinese. Some of them seem to believe that Great Britain could and would act as an outpost for our defense if Europe were overrun by enemy invaders, and submarine and aircraft bases were created on its shores. As improvisers of world strategy, the opposition leaders embolden fools to rush in where other fools have trod.

American foreign policy at this time must rest fundamentally on a judgment of the intentions of Soviet Russia, based on her behavior, especially since 1945. I do not question the adherence of Soviet leaders to what they take to be the gospel of Communism—this they have proved by staking their lives on it. But it also appears that the present régime is using this gospel to expand Russian political power. Her method is not direct military attack, like Hitler's invasion of Poland in 1939, but the fomenting of internal disorder by means of a local Communist party. This step has been followed by the creation of a left-front government, a *coup d'état* led by the Communist segment of the government, the creation of a dictatorship on the Soviet model, and a submission to the control of the Kremlin.

It was because we feared the extension of Soviet domination by this procedure until it engulfed Western Europe, and left us isolated and friendless, that we came gradually and reluctantly to think of Soviet Russia as a potential enemy instead of as a wartime ally.

When North Korea invaded South Korea in June, 1950, and this was followed by the intervention of Communist China in the following autumn, a new and more ominous situation was created. Russia seemingly had used one of her "satellites," or one of her satellites' satellites, as an instrument of overt war. At this point the United Nations, under the leadership of America, sent armed forces to defend South Korea in the name of the principle of "collective security."

It is difficult to accept an outcome in which there has been so much loss with little or no apparent gain. It would be inhumane to speak lightly of the gain as offsetting the loss, but there has been a gain, and a gain for both parties. A majority of the United Nations have shown that they have the will and the capacity to unite in defense of the principle of collective security, and they have defeated the invasion of South Korea; the new Chinese armies have earned the grudging respect of the world for their courage, and their capacity, for the first time in history, to meet modernized enemy forces from abroad on something like equal terms.

While it would be useless to use the North Korean-Chinese-Russian side of this issue as an argument against the past military operations of the United Nations in Korea, the opponent's point of view does argue against that "hardening" of American policy which now seems to be resulting from domestic political pressures. Every mitigating circumstance should be taken into consideration in defining the terms of settlement.

It would seem to be wise and just that the United
Nations should withdraw from Korea, provided the
Chinese Communists also withdraw and provided
there is an agreement to conduct Korean elections
under United Nations supervision. The United Nations, at the instigation of the United States, condemned the Chinese Communists for "aggression."
This, I think, was a blunder. The present Chinese régime does not come within the jurisdiction, either legal
or moral, of the United Nations, from which it has been
expressly excluded.* This blunder is not irretrievable.
It can be rectified by admitting this régime (or re-

* In his Message to Congress on December 1, 1950, President
Truman said, "By their action the Chinese Communist leaders
have proved themselves *lawbreakers* in the community of nations" [italics mine]; but not, I suggest, until they are admitted
to that community. It is to be noted that Communist China
has since been admitted as a party to the negotiation of a
"cease fire" agreement.

This is a highly simplified statement of the case. It takes no
account of our past mistakes, in our earlier Korean policy or in
the crossing of the Thirty-eighth Parallel and approach to the
borders of Manchuria. There is nothing to be gained by dwell-
ing on what might have been. North Koreans and Chinese
Communists have had abundant provocation. There is nothing
gained by arguing that the Korean War is a civil war, which
is not our affair. Nor is anything gained by impugning our
own motives. The stubborn fact remains that a well-equipped
North Korean army, probably with the connivance of Communist China and Soviet Russia, did, on June 25, 1950, drive
across a frontier dividing two *de facto* states; and in so doing
broke the peace.

fraining from using the veto to prevent its admission) in order that it may subscribe to the Charter of the United Nations, including the principle of non-aggression. This act would strengthen the *moral* position of Communist China herself and also our own. It is consistent with the principles and practice of the United Nations, which has not refused admission to Communist states as such, and with the policy of the United States, which has not approved the use of the veto to exclude new members.

At the same time, the United States should be prepared, through the United Nations, to permit the transfer of Formosa to whatever régime is in effective control of the Chinese mainland. This would enable those who make a moral issue of condemning the Communists* to enjoy a further sense of righteousness by fidelity to our engagements at Cairo and Potsdam where we agreed that "all the territories Japan has stolen from the Chinese, such as Manchuria, Formosa, and the Pescadores, shall be restored to the Republic of China." To adhere resolutely to this line, despite the mysterious "China Lobby," and despite the peculiar appeal of islands to the strategic imagination of the military, will require a more unwav-

*Sir Gladwyn Jebb is quoted (*New York Times,* February 2, 1951) as saying that "Now that we have established our moral position by condemning the Peiping Government as an aggressor," the most important thing was to concentrate on "an agreed solution of the Korean question."

ering leadership on the part of the Administration than it has yet dared to adopt. It is true that at the time when this agreement was made the "Republic of China" was ruled by Chiang Kai-shek, and that the present "People's Republic" is not the same republic; but neither is the present Nationalist Formosa. It is a fair assumption that the agreement was intended to assure the return of Formosa to *China*, under whatever government the Chinese people might adopt after their liberation from Japan.

In any case, a willingness on our part to concede Formosa to Communist China, in the future, if not now, through the agency of the United Nations, and provided the Peking régime stabilizes its control, is the only policy that will stand the test of time. To declare flatly that "the Peking régime is not the Government of China," and that "it is not entitled to speak for China"[2] belies our attempt to reach a negotiated settlement and stands in the way of that "Chinese-American friendship" of which our authorities continue to speak.

Some of my friends whose opinion has been accepted as the last word on Asiatic matters are prepared to "write off" China. The Chinese people, they say, now hate us so deeply, and are so indoctrinated with Communism, that it is a waste of time and effort to try to convert them. Well, I am prepared to risk wasting a little. Why do the Chinese people, who have had good reason to trust us in the past, now hate us and prefer the Communist gospel to our own? One good and sufficient reason is that we have thrown our weight against the revolution to which they are deeply committed, and of which their present leaders are the hostages. They have won this revolution *against* Chiang Kai-shek, whom we have intermittently supported.

In February, 1949, after the fall of Peking, the Communists held a victory parade, described as "the greatest demonstration of Chinese military might in history," taking two hours or more to pass, the sidewalks lined with cheering crowds. The armaments were almost *wholly American,* captured or obtained by bribery from Kuomintang forces.[3] Americans should reflect on all that this meant: triumph after years of desperate struggle; sense of victory and new hopefulness; hatred of Chiang Kai-shek as the deadly enemy; palpable evidence of our partnership with this enemy. This happened a little over two years ago; and we have done little since to alter the impression.

If, in the long run, we are to regain our once favorable position in China, we have something to live down; and the sooner we begin to live it down, the better. This, I submit, would promise better for the American future in the Far East, and for the principles we profess, than to follow the advice of "the Flying Tiger," who is quoted as recommending that China be made "a flaming hell" in order to take the Chinese "pressure off Korea." [4]

Withdrawal from Korea, and eventually from Formosa, to a line which could, if necessary, be defended without commitment of ground troops, and with the full consent of the local inhabitants, would release our resources for use in Western Europe, which we are bound to defend—bound by solemn agreement, by mutual sympathy, and by self-interest.

The problem of Germany is a special problem. We seem to be reluctant even to discuss the policy, namely, *unification-with-demilitarization,* which we have in the past professed to pursue. Why should Germany not be unified *and* demilitarized? Are we prepared to assume responsibility for the far-reaching consequences of any alternative policy? Is it that we fear that Communism would win in a free election in Germany, provided Russia agreed on an election held under adequate safeguards? Or is it that we fear that if our type of democratic régime were established in Germany, it would be overthrown by a German Communist Party supported by Russian pressure on the Eastern border? But then what of the non-Communist parties in Germany, supported, if need be, by pressure from the North Atlantic Treaty Organization on Germany's Western border?

There is not the slightest reason why the pursuit of peace by diplomatic and political means should exclude military preparations. To deny that war is inevitable, and to make determined efforts to avoid it, is not the same as to say that war is impossible or even improbable. The pursuit of peace is the line of effort; armament is the insurance against failure. It may be a credit to our hearts that war always finds us unprepared, but it is certainly not a credit to our heads. It is a matter of common prudence to be ready in advance for disasters which at the same time we seek to avert—and preparation for modern warfare has to be made in advance.

Furthermore, military strength is not only protective but deterrent. It plays an indispensable part in diplomacy; to the opponent it constitutes one of those risks which he weighs in coming to terms. Respect for another's strength serves to prolong the period of negotiation. As has been proved throughout history, weakness often invites attack, and this, being resisted, leads to counter-attack and to the mounting intensity of war.

There is little evidence that military preparedness, unless accompanied by threatening gestures, is a major cause of war. In the United States, at any rate, precisely the opposite has been the case. Those responsible for our military establishment have come to believe that the only way in which they can obtain popular support for necessary expenditures is to excite a war fever. We habitually present the spectacle of a frightened giant who has to lash himself to anger before he can rally his strength.

For this reason, public opinion has come reluctantly to the conclusion that some form of universal military training and obligation to service is advisable in the United States, at least for the immediate future. To be *habitually* in a state of readiness, or of readiness to make ready quickly when necessity arises, should render it less necessary to excite warlike passion in advance of war itself. It would also exert a steadying influence, and help to prevent the widespread panic which might otherwise be caused by the rumor or the actuality of aerial or atomic attack.

To serve its legitimate purposes, military power need not be paraded. It need not be pointed threateningly in any direction—those against whom it might be used do not need to have it pointed at them, or pointed out to them. It is not necessary to beat a tom-tom. Nor need military power be used to dominate and oppress:

> O, it is excellent
> To have a giant's strength; but it is tyrannous
> To use it like a giant.

Excessive emphasis on the military aspects of foreign policy may take many forms. It may lead to illusions of grandeur, to the prolongation of controls and regulations, to inflation and other serious disturbances of the domestic economy, to overexpenditure, and to the exhaustion of natural resources.

Of all the aspects of foreign policy, the military is

most liable to prevent the success of the other efforts. Military alliances, such as the North Atlantic Treaty Organization, might divide the world irreconcilably. The rearmament of Europe might serve to undo the effects of the Marshall Plan. The military use of wealth might seriously retard that economic and social development of the world to which we look for the widening of our own influence and the weakening of the appeal of Communism.

Above all, excessive military emphasis might bring about the very attack against which it is designed to afford protection; especially in a country such as America in which irresponsible talk is spread abroad by a sensational press. It was the Chairman of the Appropriations Committee of the House of Representatives who was reported as saying:

Moscow and every other center in Russia, we must hit within one week after the war starts. . . . In the next war, as in the last war, let us equip soldiers from other nations, and let them send their boys into the holocausts instead of sending our own boys. . . . We will blast at the centers of operation, and then let our allies send the army in, other boys, not our boys, to hold the ground we win.

"Brave, and slightly sickening talk," added the commentator who quoted the above words: weakening our efforts for peace abroad, increasing the "national war psychosis" at home, injurious to our friends, and provocative to our potential enemies.[5]

A total foreign policy will seek by diplomatic and

political means to avert war while taking reasonable precautions against its occurrence. At the same time it will embrace such propaganda, and aid to other peoples, as will fortify our moral position before the world.

CHAPTER XII

AMERICA AND THE WORLD

Propaganda, in the sense acceptable to Americans, is the effort to spread abroad the ideas for which we stand. It concerns our reputation in the world, and affects the willingness of other nations to follow our lead. We cannot be said to be greatly loved, even by our friends. To some extent this is the unavoidable effect of our power and wealth. Our power hurts the pride of those who dare not offend us; our wealth brings us the unpopularity which the benefactor always enjoys with the beneficiaries.

Owing to our freedom of speech and press, we speak with many voices, some of which are offensive to those who hear them abroad and take them to represent our prevailing attitudes. To correct this discord of voices, the Government has created a Voice of America to speak for us all. One would suppose that we for whom it speaks would be interested in what the Voice says. As a matter of fact, this is not the case. Presumably the Voice is heard abroad, but it is seldom heard at home, even by those who have the necessary short-wave instrument for its reception.

The eighty daily programs of the Voice of America[1] are beamed in thirty-three languages to all parts of the world, with a "potential audience of 300,000,-000," and an estimated listening audience of "many millions." The letters from listeners have totalled as many as 40,000 a month. The programs include news (36 percent), "analyses and features" (54 percent), and music (10 percent). They are designed to give "a true picture of American life, culture and aims." The proof of their success, is, as might be expected, more evident in other parts of the world than in the Far East and in the satellite countries of Europe.

The ideological broadcasts and "program services" supplied to other agencies comprise such topics as the following: [2] "Leninism and Stalinism," "Karl Marx on the Imperialism of the Kremlin," "A Program for Economic Purposes," "The Road to Progress—Partnership or Sabotage?" "Transplanting Democracy—The Example of Japan," "Communism and the Intellectuals," "What America Is Reading," "Forced Labor," "Monopoly Capitalism," "Is America an Imperialist Power?" "The Permanent Revolution."

The official Voice of America is designed to express the unofficial mind of America. It is only one of the channels by which this mind finds expression, and it must depend on the unity which that mind finds for itself. Every American citizen has an obligation to ask what he would say to the world if *he* were speaking for America.

In competing with Soviet Russia for the suffrage of mankind, an American will call attention to the reasons for distrusting the competitor. He will point out that Communism's self-appointed rôle as channel of irresistible historical forces excludes the sense of personal responsibility, and removes the restraints of the personal conscience. It dulls men to suffering and pity. This is at once a strength and a weakness: a strength because it makes for disciplined obedience, headlong courage, and consolidation of effort; a weakness because it is so dangerous that the rest of mankind are compelled from the necessity of self-preservation to take concerted measures against it. However excusable, the fact remains that having been bred in revolutionary conspiracy, Communists resort to secrecy, betrayal, and perjury to attain their ends and become known as the enemies of law and morality.

It may be argued further that Soviet Russia, riding on the wave of the double revolution, eventually betrays that revolution. Having delivered the workers and the peasants from exploitation by private landowners and industrial magnates, she subjects them to the harsher and more complete domination of the state, which controls not only their labor and property, but their minds and their souls. And having delivered colonies and dominions from the older and milder imperialisms, she then brings them under her own more absolute imperialistic rule.

While the older imperialisms, bad as their record is, have moved steadily in the direction of decentralization, Moscow, with its Politburo, seeks to be the seat of supreme authority for the whole Communist world. America has its allies and its spheres of influence, whereas Soviet Russia has its satellites from whom it expects undeviating obedience. The clearest proof of this is the experience of Jugoslavia, which has good reason to charge the Communist mother country with having sacrificed even the principles of Marx and Lenin to her political ambition.[3]

Anti-Communistic propaganda will be more effective in the long run if it is conducted in a spirit of fairness. In this spirit a pamphlet entitled *Toward an Integrated World Policy*, published by The Catholic Association for International Peace, recognizes that as between Soviet Russia and the West, the good does not lie altogether on the side of the latter: "The Soviet degrades the individual. On the other hand, the West does not sufficiently realize that individuals, private organizations and governments must work for the general welfare even as they protect individual rights."[4]

Propaganda, whether at home or abroad, is weakened by an excessively negative accent. We are "against Communism"—on that we are agreed, and we have left no doubt of it in the minds of other nations. Indeed, our own creed seems sometimes to mean little other than whatever Communism is against. But the best way of speaking against anything is to speak for something. Negative propaganda has the effect of intensifying the beliefs of those who already believe, and makes few converts. Hate is not an ingratiating thing; if all the world loves a lover, perhaps there is some truth in the reverse. At any rate, hate is corrupting at the source. To hate even the Devil to the extent of being perpetually haunted by him is a recognized form of primitive superstition.

Our appeal is to people and not to governments, and to people who are already indoctrinated. To many of them, to those whom we are most eager to reach, an attack on Marx and Lenin is blasphemous, as though we were to hear attacks upon Washington and Lincoln. Appeals to people to repudiate their saints and heroes, or to rise against their existing governments, will often arouse only a more intense and stubborn loyalty.

If it is well for us to acknowledge the merits of the opponent, it is also well for us to recognize, at least to ourselves, our own faults and weaknesses. Our policy sometimes smells of oil, or of some other material gain: there is no wickedness in this, provided it is candidly admitted, and subordinated to other and less sordid aims. We are the adherents of a capitalistic economy, differing only in the degree of our capitalistic orthodoxy. We view collectivism and economic planning with suspicion, and owing to political oscillations at home, we cannot boast abroad of the New Deal or even of the Fair Deal. And this occurs at a time when the revolutionary movements throughout the world are demanding instant and large-scale remedies which only collectivism and economic planning can provide, or even claim to provide. Our emphasis on personal freedom, and on free discussion, the multiple party system, and the secret ballot, does not promise the prompt and united action required for successful revolt, whether against privileged interests or against imperialistic rule.

The fact is, and we may as well admit it, that our background and our achievements are those of that "bourgeoisie" which is the hated enemy of the proletariat. We have only recently discovered, and still easily forget, that much the greater part of the human iceberg lies below the visible surface. In the minds of the revolutionaries of Asia and Eastern Europe, we are associated with that rising class which, having risen, now sits comfortably and complacently on top, and seeks to retain its seat. It is not altogether accidental that we find ourselves on the side of the Chiang Kai-sheks, the Syngman Rhees, the Bao Dais, the Quirinos, and even the Francos, tainted as they are with reaction and sometimes with Fascist or Nazi collaboration.

We are also associated with past imperialisms created by conquest and maintained for purposes of exploitation. Like landed and industrial magnates, these imperialisms have relinquished their conquests and privileges only when compelled to do so. The descendants of those whom they conquered and exploited are scattered about the globe; and they have memories, or if they don't, there are those who are prepared to create memories for them. They are seizing by violence that which their imperial masters are now tardily disposed to hand to them.

Consider the case of China. This ancient country has witnessed through the years the successful invasions of the Far East by Portuguese, Spaniards, Dutch, French, British, and Czarist Russians. They have been dispossessed of treaty ports and forced to submit to the humiliation of extra-territoriality. They have been invaded, defeated, and despised by superior armies and navies of the more advanced societies of Europe and of a Europeanized Japan. And now, having been pushed around for all these years, they find that they can do a little pushing themselves, and are disposed to push hard. This we should understand, even when we do not approve.

And present appearances are against us. We are extended over the surface of the planet in a manner that *looks* strikingly like that of the European empires. Furthermore, and this is perhaps even more important, these empires are our friends and allies. To understand Russia's view of what we call her "expansion" requires no probing into her dark Slavic soul. One force cannot come into collision with another force unless both have arrived at the same place at the same time. If our territorial claims are threatened by Russia anywhere in the world, it is because we are there, and not only because she is there. And to the simple-minded Russian, it appears from a glance at the map that the collision, if there is one, will occur nearer where they live than where we live. If we identify our boundaries with China to the west of us and with the Dardanelles on our east, it *looks,* again in a simple-minded way, as though we had succeeded to the rôle of those empires which boasted that the sun never set on their dominions. These appearances we have to take account of, if they are to be corrected.

The strength of our appeal must lie in what we are for, and not in what we are against. We must seek not to destroy the opponent's ship, but to take the wind out of its sails. It is not necessary for us to claim perfection either for our past or for our present, provided we can define a line of change that promises a better future. Here we have every right to draw not only on our record of improvement, but on our aspirations.

Despite appearances, we *are* non-imperialistic, or at least comparatively so, and in intent. We withdrew from Cuba, gave the Philippines a considerable measure of independence, and returned the Boxer indemnity to China; we have adopted a more disinterested policy in South and Central America and in the West Indies, and we have no drive toward territorial expansion and no love of domination. We are disposed to promote high standards of living in all parts of the world, old and new; this is at one and the same time our interest and our benevolent design.

We are willing to be classified as "capitalistic," but have too readily accepted the rôle assigned to capitalism by our opponents. We *are* capitalistic, but the relation between our capitalism and our democracy is, in principle if not always in practice, the reverse of that which Marxists would have the world believe. Our capitalism is the servant of our democracy. Our fundamental creed is equalitarianism—the idea that the good life, the *human* life, should be open to all so far as capacity permits; and that by early conditioning, education, vocation, and environment, capacity itself should be raised to the highest possible level throughout every part of society. We justify capitalism, insofar as we do justify it, as a means to this end: by the material goods which, by the techniques of mass production, it creates in abundance and distributes widely; and by the opportunity of individual choice which it extends to men at the bottom as well as at the top of the economic system.

These claims made for capitalism are not completely proved, and they are always on trial. The Voice of America has done well to adopt the slogan of "permanent revolution"—meaning perpetual dissatisfaction with present achievement, and continuous change in the direction of improving the condition of the less privileged classes at home and developing a "good neighbor" policy abroad. The important thing is that the accepted test is the good of all, of which one sure index is the condition of the least fortunate. Our conscience and our prudence alike forbid our being content so long as masses of mankind are denied their human birthright.

The purpose of American democracy is not to tear down but to lift up, not to abolish higher classes in favor of lower, but to put together the peculiar contributions of all classes—the leisured privileged class, the artists and scholars, the middle class of professional men, business men and farmers, and the class of those who work with their hands—and to make this sum of diverse values the common possession of society as a whole, shared, so far as possible, by all its individual members. This ideal society we hope to achieve peacefully, sparing mankind the horrors of civil war, with its bloody struggles, its executions and purges, its atmosphere of suspicion, its persecutions and reprisals.

With our social creed is joined a creed of political and civil liberty. Our system of government rests on a popular will which is arrived at through free discussion, expressed through free speech and assembly, and registered through the free ballot. We would persuade and not coerce. This creed places us against authoritarianism on the one hand, and against mob rule on the other. It is a creed designed for men in whom the rational faculties have been matured and who have in some degree acquired the virtues of tolerance, good will, and personal responsibility. We do not ourselves live up to this creed; many of our people fail to understand it, or even to remember it. But we profess it, criticize ourselves by it, and offer it to the world as a goal to be attained whenever and wherever circumstances permit.

Our foreign policy, then, must couple with diplomacy and military preparedness a ringing declaration of faith: embracing not only our firm belief in the civil liberties, and in the right of peoples to govern themselves by free elections and open discussion, but also, and with equal emphasis, our sympathy with the submerged, exploited, subjugated and otherwise relatively underprivileged, classes and areas everywhere. In other words, we must identify ourselves with the deeper purpose, though not with the methods, of the world-wide revolution of our day.

The fourth part of our total foreign policy affords us an opportunity of proving our words by our deeds —so that the voice and the hand may go together. The best name for this branch of policy is "world development." Everybody approves of it, until the time comes to make the appropriation or pay the taxes; or unless the opposite political party has first proposed it.

There are several good reasons for our participation in world development. Owing to our wealth, we have much to give, which implies a corresponding obligation. It would strengthen our moral position. It would be an application, on a world-wide scale, of our belief that the removal of poverty and misery is a preventive remedy for Communism. World development also appeals to the sentiment of humanitarianism.

Humanitarianism is a cardinal principle of American democracy: it is rooted in our tradition and fostered among us by every form of religious and moral piety. There has never been so great an opportunity for it as now—in the need, in the awareness of the need, and in the means of meeting it. But in modern times we have a somewhat different view of the matter from those which have prevailed in the past. Readers of Dickens will recall Mrs. Jellaby, who neglected her housework for the benefit of backward areas:

The African project at present employs my whole time. It involves one in correspondence with public bodies, and with private individuals anxious for the welfare of their species, all over the country. I am happy to say it is advancing. We hope by this time next year to have from a hundred and fifty to two hundred healthy families cultivating coffee and educating the natives of Borrio-boola-Gha, on the left bank of the Niger.[5]

Efforts to advance the "welfare of the species" are now more realistic and more highly organized than the Good Samaritanism of earlier days. We have not hardened our hearts against compassion, but we have come to see that a world of healthy and happy and reasonably prosperous people is a good world to live in—good for everybody, including ourselves. This does not mean that humanitarianism must "pay" merely in the sense of narrow self-interest, but, to put a fine point on it, that we prefer the kind of good for ourselves that is shared with others.

On this ground, we participate in the measures taken by the United Nations to promote education, public health, and "economic and social" progress throughout the world; and we also devise plans of our own. The idea of world development is not to help others *who* help themselves, but to help others *to* help themselves, by providing capital and technical advice, or by assisting in the construction of public works.

It makes a great deal of difference how this is done, and from what motives. There is a sinister sense in which, internationally speaking, it is more blessed to give than to receive. Giving may be a way in which imperialism gets its foot in the door. The history of the last three centuries has made the recipients of economic aid suspicious. They are inclined to believe that there is a string attached even when they can't see it. Socialist countries have reason to suspect that welfare obtained from capitalist countries is designed not to promote welfare but to promote capitalism. Or, the help given may help to make the rich richer without benefit to the people at large. Or, conditions attached to the aid may violate ways of life which are dear to the recipient. Its successful administration requires a sympathetic understanding of local customs and traditions.

These suspicions and doubts must be lived down by seeing to it that what purports to be disinterested is honestly so—not sentimentally or hypocritically charitable, or imposed in a manner that suits the giver rather than the receiver, but adapted to the interest and the autonomy of all concerned.

World development is not designed to buy military support, or to obtain "essential materials" for military purposes, whether against Communism or against any other alleged common enemy. Such operations are defensible, but they should be charged to the military account. To conceive of world development in these terms is to pervert its meaning. Its purpose is not to implement war, but to prevent it, and to raise standards of living in times of peace.

In his Inaugural Address of January 20, 1949, President Truman said:

Fourth, we must embark on a bold new program for making the benefits of our scientific advances and industrial progress available for the improvement and growth of underdeveloped areas.

More than half the people of the world are living in conditions approaching misery. Their food is inadequate. They are victims of disease. Their economic life is primitive and stagnant. Their poverty is a handicap and a threat both to them and to more prosperous areas.

For the first time in history humanity possesses the knowledge and the skill to relieve the suffering of these people.

This recommendation, now known as "Point Four," was approved by Congress in an "Act for International Development," and the sum of $35,000,000 was appropriated for its purposes.[6] In his Message to Congress on May 24, 1951, the President referred wistfully to this small beginning:

For our part, if peace could be made sure, the American people would be glad to invest a part of the resources we must now allocate to defense to a large scale program of world-wide economic development. . . . With such a program, we could, in coöperation with other peoples, inaugurate the most hopeful and fruitful period of peaceful development the world has ever seen.

This was our vision six years ago, when the war came to a close. Let us never forget it. And let us never give up our hopes and our efforts to realize it.

The vision had not been realized, owing to inertia, and to the increasing diversion of national resources and public attention to meeting the threat of war. President Truman's continued interest had been indicated by his request for a study of the subject by Gordon Gray. Then, in November, 1950, he had created an International Development Advisory Board, under the Chairmanship of Nelson Rockefeller; and in March of the following year the Board rendered its report, bearing the title, "Partners in Progress."

This report restated the argument for world development, and recognized the need for operations on a larger scale than had hitherto been proposed. It recommended the creation of an International Development Authority to which the United States should subscribe $200,000,000, in addition to $500,-000,000 to be appropriated for the use of an Overseas Economic Administration which would centralize and coördinate existing agencies devoted to such purposes. At the same time, emphasis was placed on inducing private investment to enter this field. While the immediate military and security needs were emphasized, the "vision" was not forgotten: "We dare not let down our guard and invite aggression. But we must also continue to invest in the future so that all the free peoples grow steadily stronger, even while policing the peace." [7] This is perhaps as much as could have been expected of a semi-official government document in the United States in the year 1951.

The Report of the Economic Survey Mission to the Philippines [8] revealed unsatisfactory economic conditions in these islands; conditions which, unless vigorous and comprehensive measures were taken by the United States, would deteriorate rapidly and lead to political disorder. The "Colombo Plan," reported in the autumn of 1950 by a Commonwealth Consultative Committee, and subsequently adopted by the governments concerned, provided for "development programmes" in India, Pakistan, Ceylon, and Malaya.[9]

In America, the interest in world development is reflected by the writings and speeches of private individuals. Among these, two are deserving of special mention. Stringfellow Barr, who has been connected with the Foundation for World Government, has written a highly successful pamphlet entitled *Let's Join the Human Race,* in which he advocates a World Development Authority, analogous to the Tennessee Valley Authority; and James P. Warburg, in his *Victory Without War,* has both commended and criticized the various efforts in the direction of world development made by the United States Government, beginning with the Marshall Plan.[10]

There can be no doubt of the wide interest in this matter, in America and throughout the world. The Nelson Rockefeller Report lists twenty-seven official agencies in the United States, and thirty-six worldwide organizations, "concerned with economic development"; and all these are exclusive of a very large number of "religious, philanthropic, and voluntary organizations." [11] As is usual when ideals are involved, the unofficial opinions are in advance of official policy and action. This part of foreign policy appeals strongly to the churches, Catholic, Protestant, and Jewish, and to critics, moralists, reformers and

[213]

other citizens who would like a better cause to work for than merely the defeat of Communism. They rightly protest against subordinating world development to the cold war, and against loss of faith in the constructive possibilities of the United Nations.

World development forms only a part of a wise foreign policy for the United States in the present crisis. We cannot afford to put all our eggs in one basket, even in "Operation Breadbasket." There can be no question of abandoning diplomatic and political efforts to achieve a stable peace, or of neglecting such military preparations as are required for our defense and power. We must appeal with words to the good opinion of mankind. But world development provides a way in which we can suit action to words, and devote ourselves *now* to a lasting and humane cause.

CHAPTER XIII

FORGOTTEN BROTHERS

F ree world" is a good expression. But there is a better—namely, the "human world," or "mankind." Accepting the meanings of freedom outlined in a previous chapter, "the free world" may be used to name a series of widening circles: to include only those who *are* free; or, to include also those who are aspiring to freedom; or to include those who for historical, geographical, political or other reasons are on *our side* in the present cold war—the name of "free" being given to the whole of this widest circle because its leaders belong to the first and narrowest circle.

One hesitates to name the nations which belong to these circles. But France, Italy, the Low Countries, Great Britain, Western Germany, the Scandinavian countries, Israel, the English-speaking Commonwealths, the United States, and some of the republics of Latin America would be generally recognized, or would recognize themselves, as belonging to the innermost circle. They *enjoy* freedom—by no means perfect freedom, but freedom in a comparatively high degree. The second circle would include, in addition to the above, India, Burma, Indonesia, Turkey, the new Japan, the Philippines and most of the Latin American republics. The third would add the Arab states of the Near East, Jugoslavia, Portugal, Spain, and is open to further applications.

Many of these are marginal cases, but the principle remains the same. All of these circles are exclusive. Even the name "peace-loving nations," which was adopted to symbolize the extreme hospitality of the United Nations, does not reach universality. It excludes as well as includes; or includes all only in a sense of hopeful expectancy. All classifications of mankind, save one, distinguish between some kinds of men and other kinds of men—and they usually begin with "our kind." There is only one classification that does not oppose man to man, and that is the class of all men. This is, of course, a truism, but truisms may be important and they are sometimes forgotten when it is most important to remember them.

The idea of the common humanity of all men is not, like the idea of atomic energy, or the idea of the expanding universe, a product of recent science, or a difficult idea which only the experts can understand. It is a very primitive and a very simple idea. Humanity can be seen, and is frequently seen, by any man in any other man by ignoring those differences which are thrust upon our attention by fears, rivalries, and conflicting loyalties. And in these days of world-wide communication, the concrete totality of the earth's inhabitants is brought into view as never before in human history.

Because we live in the memory of recent wars and the fear of war to come, and have been taught to consider half of mankind our enemies, it may seem inappropriate to speak of human brotherhood. But it is this ineradicable kinship that makes the present state of mankind so deeply tragic. Men are not recognized as men because of the shields they wear. I read in my boyhood, and have never forgotten, the story of Balin and Balan, two knights of King Arthur's Round Table who fought all day until nightfall when, left alone on the field of battle and both mortally wounded, they discovered that they were brothers. One of the knights makes himself known:

"My name is . . . Balan, brother unto the good knight, Balin. Alas, said Balin, that ever I should see this day, and therewith he fell backward in a swoon. Then Balan . . . put off the helm off his brother, and might not know him by the visage it was so ful hewn and bled; but when he awoke he said, O Balan, my brother, thou hast slain me and I thee, wherefore all the wide world shall speak of us both. Alas, said Balan, that ever I saw this day, that through mishap I might not know you, for I espied well your two swords, but by cause ye had another shield I deemed ye had been another knight." [1]

Human brotherhood is not a mere matter of classification. It underlies the oldest of the moralities,

[217]

namely, the *concern* of a man for his brothers. Official exponents of foreign policy feel obliged to link it with self-interest. The fact is, however, that measures designed to raise up our less fortunate fellow-men owe much of their popular appeal to a simpler and more generous motive. Humanitarianism needs no apology, even when its objects are Russians or Communists. Unless we recover that concern and feel it toward all men without exception, including those who are on the other side in every fratricidal dispute, we shall have lost the chief redeeming force in human history.

NOTES

CHAPTER I

1. E. Crankshaw, *Russia and the Russians*, 1948, p. 125.

CHAPTER II

1. Stephen C. Pepper, *Digest of Purposive Values*, 1947.
2. Ethel Waters with Charles Samuels, *His Eye Is on the Sparrow*, Doubleday & Co; 1951, pp. 93, 97.
3. Plutarch's *Lives*, trans. by A. Stewart and G. Long, Bohn's Library Edition, 1881, Vol. III, p. 376.
4. Plato, *Phaedrus*, trans. by Jowett, 1892, Vol. I, pp. 452, 460.

CHAPTER III

1. For the clarification of American political thinking the reader is advised to follow the articles of James Reston, Washington Correspondent of the *New York Times*.
2. Norman Cousins, "Conversations with Nehru," *Saturday Review of Literature*, April 21, 1951, p. 48.
3. They retain "emotional meaning," when they have ceased to have "objective meaning." The current vogue for this distinction is due largely to the influence of Charles Stevenson's *Ethics and Language*, 1944.
4. Edmund Stevens, *This Is Russia Uncensored*, 1950, p. 154.
5. Quoted in the *New York Times Book Review*, April 22, 1951.

6. *New York Times*, April 18, 1951 (italics mine).

7. *New York Times*, April 19, 1951 (italics mine).

8. Speech at a Jefferson-Jackson Day dinner in Washington, April 14, 1951; reported in the *New York Times*, April 15, 1951.

9. *New York Times*, April 15, 1951.

10. *Op. cit.*, *New York Times*, April 19, 1951.

11. Article 2.

12. L. M. Goodrich and E. Hambro, *Charter of the United Nations*, 1946, p. 71.

13. For the classification and description of these plans for world organization I am indebted to a brochure entitled *Toward Consensus for World Law and Order*, published by Duke University, 1950. All of these plans are expounded and argued by their advocates in published statements. Cf. Clark Eichelberger, "World Government via the United Nations," *Annals of the American Academy*, 264 (1949); Clarence K. Streit, *Union Now; Bulletin* of the Citizens' Committee for United Nations Reform; Cord Meyer, *Peace or Anarchy;* Grenville Clark, *A Plan for Peace* (World Federalists); Committee to Frame a World Constitution, *Preliminary Draft of a World Constitution*, published by the University of Chicago Press.

14. Testimony before the Senate Armed Services and Foreign Relations Committees, May 8, 1951; reported in the *New York Times*, May 9, 1951.

15. President Truman's Inaugural Address, January 20, 1949.

16. *New York Times*, December 29, 1950. The meaning here is closely related to that of "appeasement."

CHAPTER IV

1. *Complete Works*, ed. by Nicolay and Hay, 1902, Vol. I, p. 582.

2. This is from Jefferson's *Bill for Establishing Religious Freedom*, the original of the *Statute of Virginia for Religious Freedom*, which, along with the Declaration of Independence, was named by Jefferson as one of his proudest achievements.

3. Cited by Zechariah Chafee in his *Free Speech in the United States,* Harvard U. Press, 1941, p. 81. The passage is taken from the decision, written by Holmes, in the case of *Schenck v. United States,* 1919. It has become a highly influential interpretation of the First Amendment to the Constitution, which reads: "Congress shall make no law respecting an establishment of religion, or prohibiting the free exercise thereof; or abridging the freedom of speech, or of the press; or the right of the people peaceably to assemble, and to petition the Government for a redress of grievances" (italics mine).

4. "Address at a Sanitary Fair" in Baltimore, April 18, 1864. *Speeches and Letters,* Everyman's Library Edition, pp. 219-220.

CHAPTER V

1. Written June 9, 1788; cf. *The Writings of Benjamin Franklin,* ed. by Albert H. Smyth, 1907, Vol. IX, p. 659.

2. Written October 11, 1750; cf. New York Historical Society, *Colls., Colden Papers,* Vol. IV, p. 227.

3. Philip Blair Rice, *Kenyon Review,* Winter 1950, p. 120.

4. Clifton Fadiman, "The Passing of a Prophet," in *Saturday Review of Literature,* August 31, 1946, p. 6.

5. Giovanni Guareschi's *The Little World of Don Camillo* (trans. by U. V. Trowbridge), 1950, contains a charming statement of this idea by the priest Don Camillo to his friendly opponent, the Communist Mayor, who complained that the oratory in the public square had been interrupted by the ringing of bells from the adjoining church: "You blow your trumpets and we ring our bells. That, comrade, is democracy. If, on the other hand, only one person is allowed to perform, that is a dictatorship." (p. 61).

6. Cf. Z. Chafee, "The Press Under Pressure," *Nieman Reports,* published by the Society of Nieman Fellows, Cambridge, Mass., April, 1948, pp. 19-21.

CHAPTER VI

1. This Project is under the direction of Henry W. Holmes and James J. Mahoney, Cambridge, Mass. The Catholic University of America is editing a so-called *Faith and Freedom* series, designed for primary and secondary school pupils, and including such titles as "Our Town," "Our Nation," "Our Neighbors," etc. A text widely used in Catholic high schools is *The Christian Citizen*, by Thomas J. Quigley (1945).

2. The only survey of instruction in "civics" in American public high schools appears to be Howard E. Wilson's *Education for Citizenship*, published in 1938 and limited to the State of New York. He finds present methods, as judged by their results, to be highly unsatisfactory.

3. *Inquiry into Meaning and Truth*, 1940, p. 10.

4. *The Vanity of Dogmatizing*, 1931, p. 183.

5. Prepared by the Bureau of Applied Social Research of Columbia University.

6. Robert S. Lynd, "The Science of Inhuman Relations," *New Republic*, August 29, 1949, p. 22; a review of *The American Soldier*, Princeton University Press, 1949.

CHAPTER VII

1. Published in Edinburgh, 1946.

2. *Exodus*, 20:18.

3. *The Mill on the Floss*, Book VII, Ch. II.

4. *The God That Failed*, edited by R. Crossman, 1949, p. 228.

5. Letter to Madison, September 6, 1789; *Writings*, Ford Edition, 1895, Vol. V, pp. 115-124.

CHAPTER VIII

1. *Memories and Studies*, 1911, pp. 37-61; in *As William James Said*, edited by Elizabeth P. Aldrich, 1942, p. 145.

2. The Fulbright Report here cited is the *Interim Report*, dated February 5, 1951, and the Kefauver Report is the *Third Interim Report*, dated May 1, 1951, p. 1.

3. Robert S. Harper, *Lincoln and the Press,* 1950; summarized and quoted by T. B. Sherman, *Saturday Review of Literature,* February 10, 1951, p. 10.

4. p. 193.

5. Speech made on the floor of the Senate on March 27, 1951; *Congressional Record,* 82nd Congress, First Session.

CHAPTER IX

1. *Situation in Asia,* 1949, p. 53.

2. *New York Times,* April 15, 1951.

3. Cf. Crane Brinton, *The Anatomy of Revolution,* 1938.

4. These passages are from Cecil Woodham-Smith, *Florence Nightingale,* McGraw-Hill Book Co., 1951, pp. 30-31. The quotations are from Florence Nightingale's own letters.

CHAPTER X

1. Portions of this and the following chapters have appeared in the author's article entitled "The Logic of Peace," which appeared in the *Atlantic Monthly* for December, 1947.

2. Henry McLemore, *Los Angeles Times,* May 4, 1949. By permission of the McNaught Syndicate, Inc.

3. Quoted from a letter written by Lieutenant Charles M. Campbell, Jr., MC.

4. Speech before Jewish War Veterans, reported in an AP dispatch of April 5, 1949.

5. Churchill's speech before the Mid-Century Convocation of the Mass. Inst. of Technology, reported in an AP dispatch of March 31, 1949.

6. UP dispatch from Berlin, March 29, 1949.

7. As reported in the *New York Times,* April 20, 1951. (One apparent typographical error corrected.)

CHAPTER XI

1. *Abraham Lincoln: The War Years,* Harcourt, Brace & Co., 1939, Vol. VI, pp. 48-49.

2. These are the words of Dean Rusk, Assistant Secretary of

State, spoken on May 18, 1951, before the Chinese Institute of America. It has been referred to as a "strong speech"—indeed it was too strong for Secretary Acheson, who felt obliged to explain it away as a matter of choice of words, literary composition, etc. Cf. the news conference reported in the *New York Times*, May 24, and May 27, 1951.

3. D. Bodde, *Peking Diary*, 1950, pp. 103-104.

4. Words attributed to General Claire Chennault by Drew Pearson in his "Merry-Go-Round," *Boston Traveler*, December 28, 1950.

5. Hanson W. Baldwin's column in the *Los Angeles Times*, April 21, 1949.

CHAPTER XII

1. The following information was obtained from the Office of International Information, Department of State, to which application may be made for further details.

2. For further information concerning this branch of the work, application may be made to Voice of America, Department of State, 251 W. 57th St., New York City.

3. Cf. the speech of Milovan Djilas, Minister in the Jugolav government, in March 1950; reported in *Information Service* (published by the Federal Council of the Churches of Christ in America), September 9, 1950.

4. F. 13; published in 1950.

5. *Bleak House*, Chap. IV.

6. *Public Law* 535.

7. *Partners in Progress*, p. 9, Government Printing Office, 1951.

8. Released by the State Department in October, 1950.

9. Published by His Majesty's Stationery Office in London, and available through the British Information Services in New York City. Although this Report invited the participation of other nations, Secretary Acheson has indicated that this country would not accept; cf. *New York Times*, February 22, 1951.

10. The first of these pamphlets is published by the University of Chicago Press; the second by the Current Affairs Press of New York City. To these should be added *Steps to Peace*, by the American Friends Service Committee, and the writings of Alexander Klein.

11. Cf. pp. 118-120.

CHAPTER XIII

1. Sir Thomas Malory, *Le Morte Darthur*, 1927, pp. 75-76.